A Catholic Woman's Guide
to Relationships

A CATHOLIC WOMAN'S GUIDE TO RELATIONSHIPS

Rose Sweet

TAN Books
Gastonia, North Carolina

Cover design by Caroline K. Green

Cover image by David Shawley / Shutterstock

Library of Congress Control Number: 2020940991

ISBN: 978-1-5051-1225-2
Kindle ISBN: 978-1-5051-1890-2
EPUB ISBN: 978-1-5051-1891-9

Published in the United States by
TAN Books
PO Box 269
Gastonia, NC 28053
www.TANBooks.com
Printed in the United States of America

Contents

Part i

Standing at the Door

Behold, I stand at the door and knock; if any one hears my voice and opens the door, I will come in to him and eat with him, and he with me.

—Revelation 3:20

Introduction

Goodness gracious, there is no way one can pack in all the wisdom about healthy relationships in one little book! So I will simply begin in the way that the Gospel of John ends: "But there are also many other things which Jesus did; were every one of them to be written, I suppose that the world itself could not contain the books that would be written" (Jn 21:25).

To properly enjoy and digest something rich—and not make yourself sick—it should be served in small portions. Think of a juicy, fluffy, gravy-drenched Thanksgiving dinner; there is a little savory and sweet, starchy and salty, and maybe things that you would prefer to not even look at (that green bean casserole?)! Similarly, this book has a little of everything to whet your appetite for more.

And there is no way that you can put

3

everything good on your plate in one go-around. You *must* go back for seconds, and later for left-overs! When you're hungry for relationship truth, I hope this book is one you can go back to again and again.

In the pages that follow, I've served up some of my best recipes for love, peace, freedom, and joy in living and working with others. I got them from Jesus; savor them and give thanks to the Lord for he is good.

His love is everlasting (see Ps 136).

Entering the Interior World

*Indeed, the Architect of Love has built the door
into heaven so low that no one but a small child
can pass through it, unless, to get down to a
child's little height, he goes in on his knees.*

—Caryll Houselander, *Reed of God*

I love magic doorways.

When I say "magic," I'm not referring to superstition or the occult but the commonly used word for the mystery and allure of God's supernatural creation. I wrote more about our Catholic mysteries in the first two books of this series on happiness[1] and romance.[2]

---

[1]   Rose Sweet, *A Catholic Woman's Guide to Happiness* (Charlotte: TAN Books, 2018).

[2]   Rose Sweet, *A Catholic Woman's Guide to Romance*

We are intrigued, and sometimes scared, to discover doorways that lead us into other worlds. Ever since I was a child, I've loved to read stories of secret entrances (doors, portals, gates, platforms, and even mirrors) that opened to great adventures! Alice's tiny door into Wonderland, Dorothy's farmhouse door into Oz, and my favorite, Lucy's hidden door through the back of the English wardrobe.

Man has always longed to explore other worlds, and it's no wonder: *we were made for heaven*. God will never cease drawing us to himself (see CCC 27), and all of nature and creation is our invitation to the supernatural realm. Most especially, the Church and the Sacraments are mysterious ways of truly uniting the visible and invisible worlds of which we are all a part.

But these doors and this adventure should lead us not just to places but to Persons: into relationship with *the Father, the Son, and the Holy Ghost*. Not only do worlds meet but also hearts. Our heavenly Father wants us to discover not only his hidden secrets but mostly the abundant love he has for us. God himself is a relationship

(Charlotte: TAN Books, 2018).

of perfect love and harmony between divine Persons (see CCC 233); our relationships with others will be disastrous unless they reflect this holy communion.

Doors are more than they seem

Doors keep us safe. Funny, though, when people argue, they often slam a door in the other's face. Physical doors can also have spiritual and emotional dimensions to them.

Back in my single days, I dated a man who became increasingly frustrated that I didn't listen to him and therefore didn't understand him. Sadly, he was right. But it didn't hit me until the night he literally shut the door in my face, making sure I could hear him loudly turn the inside lock. Pathetically, I stood outside and called out for him, knocking at his door. All that did was give him the pleasure of refusing to answer. Then he went to the large living room picture window and, while defiantly staring me down, slowly lowered the blinds.

He was cruel to shut me out that way. I'll never forget how I got into my car, burst into tears, and sobbed all the way home. I'm thankful God will not slam the door in our faces. If we seek him with all of our heart, we will find him (see Jer 29:13). We must also keep the doors of our heart open to him . . . and anyone he sends to us!

God wired our brains for *connection*, but trauma rewires it for *protection*. That's why wounded, scared, or angry people have such a tough time forming healthy relationships. We each have the power to let love in or lock it out. Jesus came to us as the key to open those doors and enter into authentic love.

Jesus calls us into relationship with him

"Do you have a personal relationship with Jesus?"

The question took me aback when I first heard it on my car radio, listening to the Protestant radio program *Focus on the Family* in the mid-1970s. Every morning on the way to work, I would hear people share their inspiring conversion stories, of moving away from sinful lives to an intimate and trusting walk with the Lord.

They made me laugh, cry, and want more than ever to have a good relationship with Jesus.

I thought about it and said back to the radio, "Yes, I have a personal relationship with Jesus. I got it at baptism!"

After all, I was "betrothed" to him as a baby by my parents, confessed my sins to him when I was seven, and asked him to come into my heart and live there forever on my first Holy Communion day. I went to Mass with my parents and prayed pretty regularly, often pouring my heart out to him before I went to sleep. But that's where it ended.

One day, a Protestant friend asked me the question directly.

"Do *you* have a personal relationship with Jesus?"

Oh, no, here we go again.

She didn't wait for my reply.

"It sure doesn't *seem* like it by the way you live. All that man-made ritual and repetitive prayer you Catholics hang onto is in vain. Why do you keep trying to sacrifice him over and over at Mass? And why do you still have him hanging on the cross? He is RISEN!"

Back then, I didn't know how to respond. I felt attacked and was frustrated that I didn't have quick answers. But I am forever thankful for the question because it made me think and was the start of my journey (no, my *wild adventure!*) to go more deeply into the interior life.

We all have a personal relationship with Jesus

You could say that we all have a very "personal" relationship with the Lord in that he created us, he first loved us, and then he gave of himself so that we could have eternal happiness with him forever. It's just that too many take the relationship for granted, never respond fully, or reject it completely. It's *our* side of the relationship that is in question.

As an adult, I was still stuck in a childish relationship with him. I would call to him, usually only when I needed help and then wait and see what happened. If God didn't make things happen for me, I would just figure out a way to do it myself. I didn't know him very well, and I certainly didn't trust him as I should. I had never entered as a grown woman into the "bridal chamber" of his heart and surrendered myself, body and soul, to his tender love.

Everything changes with that kind of complete surrender. At some level, we all know it, and many fear it.

Jesus opens the door to love

One day, I told God, *Look, I want the truth and nothing but the truth. If the Catholic Church is full of error, I want to know it! If it is, I'm outta here!*

He loves those kinds of prayers.

I started reading anti-Catholic literature so that I could be familiar with the most common objections. Most of it was written by ex-Catholics who, I later found out, were deeply wounded by someone in the Church or who could not give up a particular sin that the Church condemned.

I also discovered the endless library of truth that the Church has preserved for us. I started to burn with desire for more of God and his mystery and eventually had my own life-changing conversion. When I began to realize something of how intensely God loved me, it was natural for me to respond with deeper love in return.

And all the routinely memorized Ten Commandments, works of mercy, and so many more structured prayers came flooding back into my heart, now animated with love.

Relationships are a door to heaven

It's no mystery that we crave relationship. God has revealed himself to *be* a loving relationship between divine Persons. And from that *relationship*, we were created to be in sweet, perfect *relationship* with him—and all others who end up in that embrace—forever.

We belong there. And we don't have to wait for heaven to begin to experience the safety, comfort, joy, and blessings of that *relationship*. The trouble starts when we do two things:

(1) Seek out other relationships first, on our own terms, and

(2) Turn away from our Christian religion—even slightly—and begin to reinvent our own version. If we separate truth from how we love others, we will deeply violate them and ourselves. That's why I write my books: to help people integrate the truths of our Catholic faith into the rest of their lives, to help them rightly "put religion into relationships."

Prayer is a direct doorway into the interior life.

The Mass is the supreme "front door."

And relationships, if understood properly, are also a way into discovering the greatest mystery of all.

(From the responsorial chant in the Matins of Christmas:)

O magnum mysterium! Et admirabile sacramentum!

Oh, Great Mystery and most admirable Sacrament!

Reflections

- How did you view God when you were young?
- How has your relationship with him changed, and why?
- How would you like your relationship with God to be different?

2

Exploring the Mystery

No one could suspect the intri-
cate mysteries of her heart.

—Kim Edwards, *The Memory Keeper's Daughter*

Sweet-smelling grasses and pungent pine trees grow thick and green in the breathtakingly beautiful lakeside forests of Michigan's Upper Peninsula. No one would suspect that lurking just below the surface of this postcard-pretty picture is the giant, life-sucking *armillaria bulbosa* fungus, one of the world's largest living organisms.

The 1,500-year-old fungus covers over thirty-seven acres (more than five football fields), weighs in excess of a hundred tons (the weight of about fifty cars), and is described by botanists as "roughly the texture of rotting fabric."

Ew-w-w.

Most of the giant organism lives underground. The only visible signs of it on the surface are some areas of tree rot and little sprouts of mushrooms.

My life used to be like that.

On the surface, there were signs of relationship distress and dysfunction, but I had no idea of the accumulated and intricate fabric of dreams, hopes, beliefs, fears, virtues, and vices that lay within me. My curiosity about the hidden part of myself and others soon grew. I wanted to know what was below the surface and behind the veil. The fascinating mystery of the human person was a doorway that led me tiptoeing into the interior life.

At first I sought answers in self-help books and found out that I was an enabler, a co-dependent, and was sabotaging relationships by trying to change everyone else to be like me. Yikes! I had a lot of work to do. I was *growing* up . . . but not yet *looking* up.

The popular books I read all had elements of

truth, but I still wasn't getting to the heart of the matter. Decades of self-discovery and communication skills, as helpful as they may be, can't satisfy the deepest hungers of the soul.

I had forgotten, or at least minimized, what I had first read in my little Baltimore Catechism: *that I came from God, I am destined for God, and the relationship he offers me is the most important of all.* Self-discovery apart from God-discovery is a dead end. I was still Catholic and reading some lives of the saints but, except for Teresa of Avila (who levitated) and Padre Pio (who had the stigmata and bilocated), their stories all seemed rather dull.

Naively, I approached relationships only with the latest cultural gurus to guide me, leaving my faith to gather dust in the sacristy of my local parish. And our dear Lord, who had been patiently pursuing me, let me crash and burn, take down a lot of others with me, and then mercifully cracked me over the head with life's two-by-four until I finally came to my senses.

I will forever love him for that.

Some of the problems you may have in relationships, or problems that others have, are like that monster mold in Michigan. We may be professionally coifed, manicured, and fit, with perfect church attendance and beautiful clothes with shoes to match! We might be fierce prayer warriors, hard workers, wonderful mothers, friends, or selfless volunteers . . . but just beneath the surface hides the rotting root of inordinate fear, pride, or bitterness (the root behind sustained anger, self-pity, general irritability, anxiety, or feelings of hopelessness).

Like a fungus that eventually takes over and kills its host, the unexamined and unaddressed problems we have can choke off love. Ask God to reveal if you're dealing with much bigger issues than you thought—in yourself or others—and then get some good professional counsel.

People are a mystery

Two things have intrigued and fascinated me since I was young: people and mysteries, and you have to admit we are both!

My mother used to sit us down at the kitchen table on Saturday mornings—while she smoked her Pall Mall cigarettes and drank her Folger's coffee—and explain people (the neighbors, the parish priest, and the president) and their behavior, including what she observed about each of us.

"You want to know *why* your sister hit you? You didn't listen to her and you purposely ignored her when she was trying to get your attention. Stop and think, Rosie; how do you think that made her feel? Yes, I know she can be a pest, and I will work with her on that, but you both need to apologize. Right now."

Mom should have been a therapist.

People are no substitute for God

My mother helped me to probe more deeply into my own heart, not just to admit shortcomings, but to find out why I did what I did and to understand what motivated others. Good relationships can be fulfilling, pleasurable, and make you feel secure, but they can also quickly (and wrongly) become the center of your life. St. John Paul II, in his magnificent work on relationships, *Love and Responsibility*,[3] tells us that God gave us

---

[3]   Karol Wojtyla, *Love and Responsibility* (San

each other to be a sincere gift to each other. God said, "it is not good for man to be alone" (see Gn 2:18), but it is also not good for us to hold another in the place in our hearts reserved for God alone. The Church calls this an "inordinate attachment" to someone who can never bear the weight of being our center.

The best relationship advice might be summed up in these words: *love more and fear less*. But to do that, we need to explore a little further into what "love" actually means and that fear can only be cast out when there is trust.

Do you remember the childhood story of the Gingerbread Man?

The baker carefully sifted the flour, grated the spices, and whipped the butter to create a sugary masterpiece. After the Gingerbread Man was finished baking, he tore himself off the cookie sheet and ran out the front door of the baker's house shouting, "Run, run, run, just as fast as you can! You can't catch me, I'm the Gingerbread Man!"

Out into the world the disobedient little delicacy ran. On the way, he met many strange animals, most of which wanted to eat him. He had a

Francisco: Ignatius Press, 1993).

few close calls, but he was determined and clever enough to evade them, laughing and chanting to each as he ran away, "You can't catch me, I'm the Gingerbread Man!"

But there is no happy ending to this tale; a wily fox tricked the baked goody into getting onto his back, and as they crossed a deep stream, the Gingerbread Man had to climb up closer to the fox's head. Too late! The fox flicked his head back, opened his mouth, and gobbled the cookie up. Most of us have had that experience by being betrayed by those we trusted.

Consider that God is like the baker, and we are his sweet creation. He made us for his pleasure and enjoyment, but we have run away from him to pursue other relationships first, and on our own terms.

Although he has given us other people to love and love us in return, they are part of his plan to get us in touch with our deepest desires for him. If we don't put him first, we will be foolishly running after others and may get gobbled up in the process.

"Come, let us bow down in worship, let us kneel before the LORD our Maker" (Ps 95:6).

Reflections

- What relationship book have you read that was helpful, and why?
- Have you ever (secretly) panicked in a relationship? Why?
- What behaviors in other people exhaust you?

Following the Master

Christ . . . fully reveals man to man him-
self and makes his supreme calling clear.

—*Gaudium et Spes*

Jesus offers us relationship riches

An adventure into the interior is about exploring, digging, and uncovering God's treasures. But the real riches of the spiritual life are not the blessings he has for us, as even these can distract us from the real pearl of great price: God himself.

In my book *A Woman's Guide to Healing the Heartbreak of Divorce*,[4] I first shared the story

---

[4]   Rose Sweet, *A Woman's Guide to Healing the*

of a little girl who wanted some pretty, plastic pearls.

The Pearls

Little Rachel was a cheery five-year-old who loved to go shopping with her mother. Mother always let her visit the toy aisles where she'd drool over the glittery plastic high heels, sparkling tiaras, and plastic bead jewelry. One day she saw the most beautiful white pearl necklace in a shiny foil box. They looked almost real!

"Oh Mommy! Can I have them? Please, please, PLEASE?"

Mother checked the price tag and wisely told Rachel, "Honey, these are $2.95 plus tax. You only have a dollar of your chore money left at home, I think, right? If you want to do some extra work around the house to earn the rest of the money, I will get them for you today. Deal?"

Heartbreak of Divorce (Peabody, MA: Hendrickson Publishers, 2001).

When they got home, Rachel ran to her piggy bank and shook out four quarters and a dime. Then she put on her new pearl necklace. "Mom, here's my money. Tonight, I'll ask Daddy if there's anything I can do for him. Thanks!" and Rachel gave her mom a big hug.

Rachel loved her pearls! That night she showed the necklace to Daddy when he read her a bedtime story. "They're lovely, sweetie," said Dad. "You look like a princess!"

One night after Daddy was finished with their usual bedtime story, he asked his daughter, "Rachel, do you love me?"

"YES, Daddy! You know I do."

"Then may I please have your pearls?"

"My pearls?" Rachel looked a little dismayed. "Well, you can have my plastic tiara. You know the one I got from Grandma last year. It's really pretty."

"No, honey," Dad said. "That's all right. Good night."

Every night when Daddy finished the bedtime story, he asked her the same question. "Can I have your pearls?" and every night, Rachel would instead offer him something else in her treasured collection of stuffed toys or dolls. She loved her pearls more than anything and hated to give them up.

After a while, though, Rachel could see the disappointment in her daddy's face, and she started to feel sad. Daddy was so wonderful, and she was starting to get a funny feeling in her tummy whenever she kept saying no to him. She realized that she loved him MORE than the pearls. Finally, one night, Rachel waited for Daddy to ask.

"Yes, Daddy! You can have them!" and Rachel reached under her pillow and cheerfully handed the necklace to her father.

Daddy had a surprise of his own. He smiled, got up, went to his room, came back, and gave Rachel a black velvet case. She opened it up and inside was a small strand of REAL pearls, just like Mommy's.

There are lots of layers to this simple story about trust, surrender, and God's patience with us. Too often I have clung far too fiercely to my own cheap desires and refused the precious gems of God's treasures. Have you?

Pearls of wisdom are in the Bible

In Scripture, pearls represent something of great beauty and value that can either point us higher to God or be a distracting substitute:

- *In the parable of the "Pearl of Great Price," our relationship with God is set above all others.* "Again, the kingdom of heaven is like a merchant in search of fine pearls, who, on finding one pearl of great value, went and sold all that he had and bought it" (Mt 13:45-46).
- *Matthew again references pearls to all that is holy—including, I may add, our own beautiful dignity and worth.* "Do not give dogs what is holy; and do not throw your pearls before swine, lest they trample them under foot and turn to attack you" (Mt 7:6).
- *In the Old Testament, Job tells us that the virtue of wisdom is something to be sought and*

treasured. "No mention shall be made of coral or of crystal; the price of wisdom is above pearls" (Jb 28:18).

In this book, I want to gift *you* with some real pearls of wisdom that God gave me, and for later reference, they're summarized on a chart at the end of this book. In Scripture, I've uncovered four easy-to-remember "relationship rules" that have far more value to me today than any precious gem. I've memorized them and they are my go-to solution for properly responding in every—yes, every—relationship. From the story of the rich young ruler who went to Jesus for answers:

> And as he was setting out on his journey, a man ran up and knelt before him, and asked him, "Good Teacher, what must I do to inherit eternal life?" And Jesus said to him, "Why do you call me good? No one is good but God alone. You know the commandments: 'Do not kill, Do not commit adultery, Do not steal, Do not bear false witness, Do not defraud, Honor your father and mother.'" And he said to

him, "Teacher, all these I have observed from my youth." And Jesus looking upon him loved him, and said to him, "You lack one thing; go, sell what you have, and give to the poor, and you will have treasure in heaven; and come, follow me." At that saying his countenance fell, and he went away sorrowful; for he had great possessions.

And Jesus looked around and said to his disciples, "How hard it will be for those who have riches to enter the kingdom of God!" And the disciples were amazed at his words. But Jesus said to them again, "Children, how hard it is for those who trust in riches to enter the kingdom of God! It is easier for a camel to go through the eye of a needle than for a rich man to enter the kingdom of God." And they were exceedingly astonished, and said to him, "Then who can be saved?" Jesus looked at them and said, "With men it is impossible, but not with God; for all things are possible with God." Peter began to say to him, "Lo, we have left everything and followed you." Jesus said, "Truly, I say to you, there is no one who has left house or brothers or sisters or mother or father or children or lands, for my sake and for the gospel, who will not receive a hundredfold now in this time, houses and brothers and sisters and mothers and children and lands, with persecutions, and in the age to come eternal life." (Mk 10:17–30)

As I read, it struck me: with this man and so many others, Jesus gives us a simple four-step pattern to follow:

Listen

No matter who approached him or why, Jesus gave each person his full attention and was able to see past the obvious and into the heart. This gave him the information or understanding he needed to respond to each person appropriately. *How many of us talk first and listen last?*

Lead

Jesus knew where each person needed to go, and he did or said whatever was necessary to help get them there. He knew how to accompany, teach, encourage, challenge, wait, and counsel in the right spirit. And, yes, rebuke when necessary. *How many of us like to start with* that *one first?*

Love

Love enabled the Lord to stand firm and not compromise on the fullness of truth, no matter how hard it was for others to hear or accept. Love also kept him from imposing his will on others, allowing them the full freedom to follow him or walk away. *How often do we back off on what is right, necessary, or true to keep another from rejecting us or walking away?*

Let go

Jesus exhorted others, got angry at injustice, and cried at loss, but then he was able to let go. He didn't stay angry, become bitter, or engage in long-standing feuds—he was always at a deep and supernatural peace. He worked hard to heal people, but when he was exhausted, he left everyone to go find rest in the Father. *How many of us lose sleep, suffer stress, or chase others down with pleas, bargains, compromises, threats, or worse?* It's difficult to let go.

With the rich young ruler, Jesus *listened, led* him to the truth of Scripture, and then called him to go farther, deeper, higher. Because of *love*! But when the man walked away, Jesus did not hunt him down. I do think, though, Jesus may have prayed for him and given him some time and space as he does with so many of us. Maybe the Holy Spirit worked overtime on the man and, six months later, he had a large going-out-of-business sale, packed a small bag, and left to join Jesus and the other disciples. Someday we will find out.

If you find the treasure, you will be a treasure to others

Jesus shows us how to *Listen, Lead, Love,* and *Let Go* with others, but he first follows these "rules" himself in his relationship with the Father.

Jesus *listened* to the voice of the Father.

Jesus allowed the Sprit to *lead* him into the desert to prepare for his work.

Jesus opened to receive the *love* of the Father and loved him in return.

Jesus *let go* of his own will in trust and obedience to the Father.

We, too, must live these four rules simultaneously, like a double strand of pearls!

Listen to God . . . so you can properly listen to others.

Let God lead you . . . so you can appropriately lead others.

Let him love you . . so you can fiercely love others.

Let go of pride and fear . . . so that you can be at peace.

Reflections

- What pearls of wisdom would you most like to give to your children or grandchildren?
- Which is easiest for you? Listen, Lead, Love, or Let go?
- Which is most difficult, and why?

PART 2

Listening

And a voice came out of the cloud, "This is my Son, my Chosen; listen to him!"

—Luke 9:35

4

Learning to Listen

Your secrets are safe with me. I wasn't even listening!

—Anonymous

Everyone agrees that listening well is a must for success in relationships. For some, listening well comes naturally. But some people listen and never hear. Distractions, selfishness, laziness, pride, and fear are like invisible earplugs that block the ears of their heart.

Listening takes time and practice

"Rose, I'm telling you, I was *so* embarrassed . . . and scared!"

My sister, Malia, had been walking down the street in her San Diego neighborhood when, all

35

of a sudden, her legs went weak, gave out, and she crumpled to the sidewalk.

"For a long time, I just sat there looking at the dirty pavement and all the old gum; I couldn't make my legs work."

I listened, imagining what it would be like to be sprawled out like that, feeling vulnerable and powerless, and having strangers gawking and walking by.

"After that, I went to the doctor right away and he told me I had a degenerative nerve disease. He said it would likely get worse and I needed to get a service dog. So, I did. He's a yellow lab and I just love him. I named him Armani."

"Armani?" I asked.

"Yeah, because he was so expensive!"

We both laughed.

"Rose, he's the best. Once, I was in the Macy's restroom and I could not get up off the toilet. Now that's pretty embarrassing and scary, too, but all I had to do was call out, *Armani, come*! He'd been trained to scoot under the metal door, brace himself against it, and help pull me to my feet. He has literally saved me on countless occasions."

I was speechless, which is good when someone else has a story to tell.

"But he wasn't much help at first. It was a long
haul to get that boy trained!"

Over six months to be exact. Malia explained
the program the trainers called FOG: Fear Of
God.

"I had to become Armani's 'god' . . . only I
fed him, only I petted him. Only I cared for him
and supplied all his needs. Only I disciplined
him. He lived with me, slept in the same room
with me, and I gave him daily walks. We spent
every day together getting to know and trust one
another. He had to develop a healthy fear and
reverence for me so that when I called him, he
would immediately respond to the sound of my
voice."

Armani was learning how important it was to
listen.

After the intense training, came graduation
day, and Armani had to be tested. Could he rise
to the high standards required of him? Since his
service to Malia might mean life or death, would
he respond immediately and obediently to her
commands?

"The trainer and his assistant took us to a busy mall, crawling with kids who love and want to pet dogs. There were loud noises and a million tempting smells. The test was *could Armani listen to my voice and ignore every distraction and come immediately to me?*

"What happened?" I asked.

"Well, before I tell you, I was instructed to stop feeding Armani the day before. He hadn't eaten in over twenty-four hours and he was starving!"

"Ahh, poor guy."

"And the trainer stood with Armani on the leash, and when I called, Armani was to ignore everything and everyone and come right to me. But the assistant had just dropped three juicy, raw steaks on the mall floor between Armani and me."

When Malia called her command, "ARMANI, COME!" the dog eagerly left the trainer and headed straight for Malia, until he got to the first steak. Looking at it, then drooling, then almost licking his chops, he looked up at Malia who urged him on. He kept going. He even made it past the second steak. But finally, when he got to the third, his hungers were too intense, and he took his eyes off his master and stopped to fill his belly.

"He flunked?"

"He flunked!"

"We had to go back to training. It was grueling. But then we had graduation again."

"Same mall, same steaks?"

"Yep. But this time he came right to me. He didn't even look down or away once. Rose, he kept his eyes on me, and when he got to me, I hugged him as hard as I think I ever had."

I couldn't help myself: I knew at once that this was a "parable" for the soul who needs to listen for her master's voice and keep her eyes on him. To trust him so much that she bears with the painful, unsatisfied hungers to come when he calls. To know that she doesn't have to feed herself in her own way and own time when he promises to meet her needs in other, even better ways.

Armani *listened*, let Malia *lead* him and *love* him, and he *let go* of the appetites and distractions that would pull him away. Don't let your relationships go to the dogs. Be Armani!

You can develop good listening skills

Here's an exercise in listening, modified from one I've used in seminars and retreats. You'll either love it or hate it, but I promise if you will practice this within your family, you'll help to create deeper trust, safety, and love in all your relationships at home. And you'll be teaching your children invaluable listening skills.

Unpacking your emotional suitcase

On our "Adventure into the Interior Life," we all bring an invisible suitcase, packed with dreams, hopes, fears, and emotions that can fester, build, or blow at any time. Just as if you were on a long safari, you should regularly open the suitcase to launder or air everything out to keep it fresh and clean.

Step 1

Two people find a quiet and private place to talk for fifteen to thirty minutes. Bring tissues.

Step 2

Person A (you) asks four questions of Person B. The questions are below, but first some necessary ground rules.

Step 3

After asking Question 1, Person A remains *silent*. No talking, commenting, affirming, adding, clarifying, etc. *As Person B begins to open up more deeply, this may be very difficult.* Remember, your job is to *just listen*.

But you're not a robot either. You may, and should, have direct eye contact. You can smile, nod, laugh, take a deep breath, cry, say mm-mm, or groan. *But no words.* They can comment on their own answers, but you can't. This is an exercise in mastering your need to affirm, fix, control, solve, or have your own say.

Step 4

The questions can seem embarrassing and invasive, but the goal is to create a safe and unhurried place for the person to think and express themselves. Many will be uncomfortable (a) going too deep or (b) saying what they think and feel out loud. We are afraid of being judged, controlled, criticized, or shamed. Some things, too, we don't like to admit to ourselves!

In order to create the optimum environment for Person B to open up, Person A pauses after each answer, asks "Is there anything else?" and then waits, giving the person time to think and share more. Some may need an additional, gentle, "Are you sure?"

When the person is finished, go to the next question and repeat the process. Typically, this will last from ten to twenty minutes. Hopefully longer if needed.

Caution: You may know they have much more to share and are holding back, but it is not your job to make this happen. Don't help them. Let it go for now. Keep doing this exercise every month or so until trust is earned, fear diminishes, and the person opens up more. And you (Person A) will be learning that it is okay to just *listen* and not fix.

Questions

They are asked in this particular order for a reason. The first questions can elicit the most painful emotions of hurt and grief, which need to be unpacked first, allowing room for the happier thoughts at the end. The last question is meant to bring them to gratitude and peace.

Person B should be free to go to any place, event, situation, reality, or relationship for their responses. Hopefully, their answers will progress from the small and exterior to the significant and deeply personal.

1 – What makes you *angry*?
(*people who cut me off in traffic, snotty store clerks, my husband's pornography addiction . . .*)

2 – What makes you *scared*?
(*spiders, loud noises, people with guns, the government, that I won't get a job, won't get married, that I will die alone . . .*)

3 – What makes you *sad*?
(*sad movies, lonely people, the state of the Church, my child who left the faith, my spouse who is depressed, that I never had children . . .*)

4 – What makes you *happy*?
(Christmas, my birthday, my beautiful home, gorgeous sunsets, music, being Catholic, Jesus in the Sacraments . . .)

Step 5

When you're finished, take a break. Hug if appropriate. Optional: Ask Person B if he/she would be willing to trade places and ask you the same four questions, either now or at some future time.

Reflections

- What distracts you most from your time with God?
- Do you think you're a good listener? Why or why not?
- In relationships, what things make you happy?

5

Hearing with the Heart

*The ear of the leader must ring with
the voices of the people.*

—Woodrow Wilson

We don't listen because we don't want to

Balaam was a prophet who was sent to God's people with a crucial message. He had been given strict instructions by God to do only what God commanded him. Frustrated with waiting, he arose one morning, saddled up his donkey, and rode off on the mission without listening for God's instructions. God was angry (see Nm 22–24).

To divert Balaam from his plans, the Lord sent

a mighty angel with his sword drawn to stand in the middle of the road. Balaam didn't see the angel, but his donkey did, so the donkey veered off into the field. Balaam used a stick to beat her to get her back on the road. Two more times the donkey saw the angel and tried to change course, but Balaam, still blind and deaf to what God was trying to tell him, beat her each time.

Obviously the angel was not enough, so God allowed the donkey to open her mouth and speak audibly to her master. The poor donkey begged him to consider how she had always been faithful and would never steer her master wrong. When a shocked Balaam stopped to think about it, he realized she must be right. Suddenly his eyes were opened, he saw the angel standing before him with drawn sword, and he dropped in terror to his knees. God had his attention now, and Balaam finally changed course.

Listening well to others is a loving act, but our primary mission is to first listen and hear the voice of God in our lives. You may be struggling in a relationship and about to embark on a path you think is wise or are otherwise headed off in some wrong direction. Maybe someone close to you sees a better way and is trying to tell you. Is it a friend, a counselor, or your pastor? Stop and listen, or God may have to put a sword in your path.

Listening requires humility

My little four-year-old niece, Sara, stood at my front door one Saturday morning, her mother (my sister, Barb) standing close behind her with one hand gently placed on her daughter's shoulder.

"Good morning, Rose," Barb said cheerfully. And, getting right to business, she continued, "Sara has something she would like to say to you."

I was surprised to look down and see little Sara clutching her pink Hello Kitty purse and wearing a serious and somewhat distressed look on her face.

With my many nieces and nephews, I had always been known as the aunt who joked and teased and gave them funny little nicknames. I wasn't ready for what Sara said.

"Aunt Rosie," she said timidly but

determinedly, "I really don't like it when you call me Whiny Torres."

What? I thought. *Well, she* was *whiny!* Practically all the time. I loved her dearly, but (blame it on my natural temperament) my immediate reaction was to make some silly crack or otherwise make light of it. My sister shot me a knowing glance before I could open my mouth.

I remembered that Sara by nature is a sensitive soul. She loves deeply but also can get acutely wounded at offenses.

I bit my lip, knelt down to her eye level, and gave Sara a sincere look of love.

"Sara" I said, lowering my voice down to a soft, introverted tone. "Thank you for telling me. I'm so sorry. Will you please forgive me?"

"Yes," she squeaked out.

I hugged her.

"I love you, honey."

"I love you, too, Aunt Rosie."

"Okay! Why don't you guys come in for some *Sara* (smile) Lee coffee cake I just pulled out of the oven?"

My sweet niece just needed me to be present and *listen* to her. Then I could *lead* her to a place of feeling understood and *loved*, and both of us could *let go*.

It was also a memorable lesson to me that even young children can learn to speak for themselves when we help them find their voice. Barb is still a smart mom of five, all grown and with children of their own. Back then, she was learning about codependent behaviors in relationships and the beauty of helping people navigate their own way with others rather than enabling them.

Humility is vital to *listening*, *leading*, *loving*, and *letting go*. In humbly listening to Sara in her "native language," I was able to make her feel loved. The memorable incident endeared me to my sister and my niece more deeply and is one of the funny but important family stories we sometimes tell at reunions.

Listening can lead to truth

I love all my nieces and nephews! Barb's oldest daughter, Alethea, was single and in her early twenties when she shared her dream with me:

"I was walking along eating an ice-cream

cone. Ice cream is my favorite treat!" she said with a huge grin on her dimpled face.

"It was so good, and I was so-o-o happy. All of a sudden the ice-cream scoop fell out of the cone and onto the ground into a pile of dirt, rocks, and fresh manure. I stood there looking at the ice cream and thinking, *Oh NO!*

I hated to admit I still wanted it. I examined it and noticed it wasn't totally covered and maybe . . . but then I thought to myself, *No, Alethea, that's disgusting!* and tried to walk away.

But I couldn't. I wanted it. Aunt Rose, I stood there fighting with myself to pick it up and eat it or walk away."

"E-w-w-w! Alethea, that *is* disgusting! What did you do?"

Alethea looked at me with horror and admitted, "I ATE IT!"

We screamed in unison and both dissolved into laughter.

Up to this point I was quietly listening and also noticing the joy and desire in her voice when she talked about loving ice cream. I saw the shock, dread, and shame on her face in wanting to eat the filth-covered scoop anyway. I knew there was much more to this dream—as there usually is.

I told my niece I thought it was very clear. She'd been dating a young man who was smart, handsome, and charming, and who adored her. But he was also pressuring her to have sex, disrespectful of her deepest desires, and letting her know he was not into marriage. Alethea admitted she loved the flattery and attention of the relationship; in fact, she was starving for it, but she knew it would make her sick if she stayed in it. Deep down, she knew that too.

I understood my niece because in the past I, too, had tried to make relationships that were not good for me work out somehow. I didn't listen to God's voice or my conscience.

We need to practice "deep listening," the kind that God does with us. The Lord will speak to you through your dreams if you don't listen to him when you're awake.

Reflections

• What is God trying to tell you right now?

- Who in your family has been a good listener to you?
- What keeps you from being a better listener?

6

Listening in Silence

Wisdom is the reward you get for a lifetime of listening when you'd have preferred to talk.

—Doug Larson, columnist and editor, *Door County Advocate*

"Hey, Honey," I hollered to my husband, "did the neighbor's property close escrow yet?"

I passed him sitting in the living room on my way to the kitchen for a quick snack. All I wanted was a *yes, no,* or *not yet* answer.

"Well . . . last week or, no, it was Tuesday . . . did I tell you the seller had his daughter fly out to look at the property? There might be a problem with the air conditioner, and they want the buyer to pay for it. You know in California property sells 'as is.' I think she lives somewhere up near Portland, I think it's Eugene, you know, where your friend Cathy lives. Not the daughter that we met when they listed the property, she's having a baby . . . their fourth!"

My eyes started to glaze over.

"*Honey . . .*" I said.

"Okay, okay, yeah. Um, I called Breeze Air Conditioning because Priority One never returned my calls. So it looks like a $3,000 job that they may have to split . . ." and on he went.

I used to want to scream, but now I get it: my husband *loves* to talk.

And I need to be willing to listen.

Some people are talkers and others are not

It's a myth that only women are chatty. Bob is a peaceful phlegmatic temperament, which means he loves to sit back, relax, and quietly watch, observe, make mental note, and take inventory. He finds life and people extremely interesting. He is bright, intelligent, and articulate.

His secondary temperament (and I will be writing more about the nature of temperaments in the next book in this series) is the passionate melancholy. He loves art, music, politics, philosophy, depth, detail, and *conversation*, where he often strays off the direct path and far out into the weeds.

I'm the opposite: a quick, get-to-the-point, no-time-to-waste choleric. I like to look out along the horizon rather than stay stuck in the details. When we're walking down a street together, I move at a fast clip while he moseys along. My eyes are on the destination and he is enjoying the journey of going in and out of all the little shops.

So, in listening to him, I sometimes get lost and frustrated. And impatient.

Me: *Hurry up! Get to the point!*

Him: *Calm down! Why are you in such a hurry?*

But—funny—our roles are reversed when he is not really interested in what I have to say, regardless of how little words I use. Personalities play a role in the way we talk or listen, but desire trumps temperament. People listen because they are interested—or not. How have I learned to listen to Bob and others like him better?

I . . .

- take a breath and remind myself that (a) listening to him is an act of love and (b) I love him!
- become as physically and emotionally present to him as I can in the given circumstance.
- wait for him to finish and do not interrupt.
- communicate silently, with nods, smiles, or other non-verbal ways to let him know I am paying attention.
- take notes. Especially when the conversation is long, it helps me remain silent and attentive while making sure I got everything that is important. Later I can confirm, comment, or add my own thoughts. (Bob's okay with the notes.)

Do I always *want* to do all this? No, of course not. I struggle with selfishness like we all do. But with God's grace and continued practice, it has become much more natural for me. And when I can listen quietly without adding, correcting, commenting, or trying to "dialogue," he feels listened to and loved.

You can't listen when you're busy talking

Most people just want someone to *listen* to them.

They don't want to be *led* anywhere, afraid of losing control or independence.

They don't want your "*love*" because, again, they misunderstand and are afraid of your intrusion into their life.

They can't *let go* of fear.

So simply listening and affirming that you hear is a way to lead them to a place of feeling safe with you, of your showing them love, and a way for you to let go of any over-responsibility.

Keeping quiet is vital to good listening—there is power in silence.

There is life and death in the tongue (see Prv 18:21)

It's tempting to talk back, argue, or criticize. It can feel good to gossip or badmouth people. While part of healthy relationships is being able to safely "tell your story," you must keep character assassination out of the pages. God's Word warns us of the sins of the tongue:

- the *lying tongue* (see Prv 6:17),
- the *manipulative tongue* (see Ps 5:9),
- the *proud tongue* (see Ps 12:3, 4),
- the *swift tongue* (see Prv 18:13),
- the *slandering tongue* (see Rom 1:30),
- the *tale-bearing tongue* (see Prv 18:8),
- the *cursing tongue* (see Rom 3:13–14),
- the *piercing tongue* (see Prv 12:18),
- and even the *silent tongue* (see Eccl 3:7).

Exactly how can you control your tongue? Well, I'm no cardiologist, but I believe there is a direct metaphoric link between the muscle we call the tongue and the muscle we call the heart. What's in the heart inevitably comes out of the mouth. If you have any bitterness, anger, or a wounded spirit from relationships, it will be revealed in the way you speak to or about others, or in the seething quiet where you refuse to speak at all.

Controlling the tongue, therefore, starts with healing the heart. Genuine kindness in our hearts is a healing balm to others, poured out in our words of affirmation, support, truthfulness, and forgiveness. Proverbs 16:24 says, "Pleasant words are like a honeycomb, sweetness to the soul and health to the body." And sometimes *silence* is the sweetest sound of all.

In the beautiful offertory prayers of the Traditional Latin Mass, the priest asks God to make him worthy to utter his prayers, making them as pure, fragrant incense wafting up to heaven.

> *Pone, Domine, custodium ori meo, et ostium circumstantiae labiis meis: ut non declinet cor meum in verba malitiae, ad excusandas excusationes in peccatis.*

> Set a watch, O Lord, before my mouth, and a door round about my lips, that my heart may not be inclined toward evils words (Ps 141:3–5).

But silence is not good when we use it to control or hurt others. When there is a life-threatening emergency or someone is in danger of serious sin, we must "cry out with a thousand voices," as St. Catherine of Siena said.

Virtue can tame the tongue

It's difficult to be silent when our emotions are running amok. Like beloved pets, our thoughts and feelings belong to us, but we must master them. "They" can sit in front of the fireplace and nap, frisk playfully around the yard, or even purr in contentment. But other times, driven by our desires and fears, our emotions can bark at others, snap at their heels, and even attack.

In those times, our intellect and will often need to keep our emotions on a short leash. In high stress situations, some of us may even need a muzzle or, God forbid, a shock collar. We can't keep emotions—or our tongue—locked up in a dark dungeon, but they must stay under our control. We shouldn't neglect, stuff, or deny emotions either, but we also shouldn't indulge them or cater to their every demand.

My friend Karen is a good example for us all. She keeps her rambunctious Tibetan terrier Barney under control by making sure:

He knows who is boss

We can remind ourselves in times of great emotional upheaval that we are in charge even if we don't feel like it at the moment. Self-control is one of the fruits of the Holy Spirit. Pray for it and practice it. Seek forgiveness when you lose it.

He never gets too tired, stressed, or nervous

The old Weight Watchers motto to help people from binging was "HALT! Never get too Hungry, Angry, Lonely, or Tired." Those states predispose us to losing control mentally, emotionally, and physically. Karen knows her pet's unique signals; we should stay in touch with what is bothering us too. Maybe we just need a nap!

She avoids places where it will be almost impossible for him to not go nuts

Call it "avoiding the near occasion of sin." Don't go places or be with people when high emotions can be triggered. If you do, bring that "leash" which are mechanisms for helping you rein it in. Walk away. Hang up. Say nothing. You don't have to attend every argument to which you are invited! Just stay home.

She checks regularly for underlying
health problems that need fixing

When people verbally attack, they are afraid or in pain. Others stuff their fears or resentments into a deep, dark place where cancerous tumors grow. Take your interior life's temperature. Check your emotional pulse. Examine your conscience. Be honest. Uncover the root of your dark or raging emotions, get to confession, and get help if necessary.

So, what will the woman holding the leash do with her feelings? Emotions can be taken up into the virtues or perverted by the vices (see CCC 1767). With God's grace, some skills, and practice, it's up to us.

Reflections

- Are you more of a talker or listener?
- Which of those Psalms or Proverbs struck you the most and why?
- Do you interject, comment, or otherwise interrupt when someone is talking?

PART 3

Leading

Don't follow the crowd. Let the crowd follow you.

—Margaret Thatcher

7

Understanding Your Role

Be who God meant you to be and
you will set the world on fire.

—St. Catherine of Siena

Freddi Dogterom, my friend who lives in Canada's Arctic, told me a fascinating story of large stone figures called Inukshuks (in-OOK-shook):

"The Arctic is a breathtakingly beautiful but potentially dangerous place to live," she shared. "Of all the dangers, including wild beasts, the most feared is probably getting lost out on the tundra. A person could wander for days until a predator or exhaustion killed him.

In the Arctic, above the tree line, the land is flat with no trees or landmarks to mark the way.

65

Forget a compass; the magnetic North Pole makes it useless. Since the population is sparse and the terrain inaccessible, there are no roads, and therefore no road maps."

Getting lost? I live in the hot Southern California desert where we literally have cactus, tumbleweeds, and road runners. And paved streets. With street signs and traffic signals. Lots of them. This place sounded way too cold and uncivilized for me.

"There's no AAA in the Arctic, Rose. It's *very* easy to get lost."

I laughed, but realized it was no laughing matter. Brrr-r-r!

"An Inukshuk is a pile of stones made to resemble a human form," she explained.

"The Inuit natives would build these stone figures to help others find their way. Sighting an Inukshuk was a great source of comfort. Because they resemble people, they are called 'Living Stones.' In the Inuit language, Inukshuk means 'Stone Man Who Points the Way.' "

I thought immediately of the ways in which we can run from predators or die from exhaustion in relationships; how we can get lost in the empty wilderness of fear and sorrow. God points the way for us through a trusted friend—a strong and steady Inukshuk he builds just for us.

"I have taught you the way of wisdom; I have led you in the paths of uprightness" (Prv 4:11).

Every leader is unique

An old Inuit woman, Ida Aleekuk, taught Freddi how to sew leather and fur and to bead *mukluks*, high boots made from the skin and fur of a moose, caribou, or seal. Ida also taught her how to build an Inukshuk.

"Each stone is carefully selected and placed in a particular order," Ida told Freddi. "Don't just go for the pretty ones. You need strong ones that will fit and give support. The headstone is the most important one of all. It defines the character of your Inukshuk." Freddi spent many hours with Ida and made hundreds of Inukshuks.

"Each figure was unique, each one special in its own way," said Freddi. "Soon they were not just a pile of stones to me. Surprisingly, my Inukshucks became like real people. Some were big, some little, some sturdy, and some weak. I made plain ones and pretty ones, but each was special."

Years later when Freddi moved, Ida gave her advice about friends. "Build a new Inukshuk but build it with new friends. Just like picking the rocks, pick each one with care. They will be your living stones. Pick some for strength, some for support, and some to fill in gaps in your life. Your new Inukshuk will help point the way."

Good leaders know where to go

Everyone leads in a slightly different way, according to age, maturity, temperament, culture, and experience. But all good leaders know this:

> *In every relationship, you have the responsi-*
> *bility to lead the other to a safe place.* Not
> a sanctuary where they never feel pain or
> discomfort, get their own way, and where
> you cater to their every demand; instead,
> a sanctuary (a holy place) where you:

- see and hear and are present to them,
- uphold their dignity as being made in God's image,

- desire what's truly good for them, primarily heaven,
- will never use them as an object to meet your needs,
- accept them for who they are without tolerating sin,
- allow them an appropriate voice,
- share, teach, guide, encourage, rebuke, or otherwise lead them to Truth,
- and are willing to accompany and even suffer to help get them there.

You can't lead safely without boundaries

In my early twenties, I lived in San Diego with my roommate Vicki. On weekends when the beach weather was cold and damp, we'd stroll through antique stores or stay home, bake chocolate chip cookies, and watch old movies.

"Let's go to Mexico!" said Vicki one Saturday morning.

Mexico? I had never been there, and back then, it was still a little scary. It was a foreign country, after all, and it was supposed to be pretty rough.

"Come on! My friend at work said there is

great shopping on Avenida Revolución, plus we can get *real* Mexican food. It will be fun!"

Yum. Mexican food, my favorite!

But, honestly, she had me at shopping.

Off we went on a foreign adventure, and in less than thirty minutes, we had crossed the border into Tijuana. I was driving and was excited at the charming and colorful old town area, until we almost got sideswiped by a huge cattle truck and killed on the spot.

What the? I panicked and quickly realized there were no lanes in the streets, no stop signs at the intersections, and no traffic signals. Without painted lines and speed limit signs, drivers were speeding, crossing in front of others, slamming on brakes, and veering into other's paths. It was a dangerous nightmare.

As a result, I had to drive extremely slowly wherever I went. I was constantly looking out the front, to the back, and both sides. I was stressed and anxious, not to mention we had not purchased temporary auto insurance. Stupid me; I hadn't thought we needed it. It was no fun at all.

We finally parked safely and then washed

down some tasty tacos with an ice-cold beer at the Long Bar. We listened to lively mariachis and spent the day shopping along the avenue and in quaint underground stores. Except for the hellish driving, it was a most excellent adventure.

That day I began to appreciate rules and regulations. It's natural for young people—and some who have not grown up—to resist, and even resent, rules. They don't like to be told what to do. They hate being restricted in any way. But boundaries aren't set to inhibit freedom; they are there to protect it.

Back in the US, yes, the yellow and white lines in the road restricted me in a sense, but staying within them gave me the freedom to go much faster than I could in Mexico. I felt safer knowing that when others stay in their lanes, we can all enjoy the ride that is life.

In relationships, you must set appropriate boundaries to keep everyone safe. In my second book in this series, *A Catholic Woman's Guide to Romance*, I write about the relationship lines that should never be crossed, the U-turns we may need to make, and times we must hold up our hand and say, "STOP!"

Rather than an act of tyranny, setting and enforcing boundaries is an act of love. If you've ever been "sideswiped" in a relationship, I'm sure you will agree.

Sometimes leaders must be tough

"I hate you!"

"You're mean!"

I've heard some children, and those who still act like children, spit these words out when they don't get their way. The real struggle for many is not the setting of boundaries, *it's enforcing them.* Why? When you enforce a boundary, you're likely to lose someone's approval, affection, or loyalty in the process. You may also be forced to create conflict and upset the peace that you crave. There's nothing wrong with desiring these, but you can be overly attached to them to the point you lose your center. Instead of you being in charge, the other person controls you.

If you cannot enforce boundaries, you are training the other person to ignore, dismiss, or disrespect you and what you are attempting to teach them. You have traded your desires, ideals, and values—maybe even your morals—to keep the peace or stay in good-standing in someone's eyes.

This might not be a big deal when you're trying to make a six-year-old make her bed, but what happens when you try to teach her to avoid serious sin? She is not likely to listen to you then either.

Gary Richmond, author of *It's a Jungle Out There*,[5] is a former veterinary assistant at the Los Angeles Zoo who once observed the birth of a baby giraffe. The mother giraffe was giving birth standing up, her hindquarters nearly ten feet off the ground, when the calf's front hooves and head came out.

Gary—worried that the baby would be hurt falling from such a height—asked if someone should go in and help.

"Stand back, Gary!" warned the vet. "That mother giraffe has just enough strength left in her legs to kick your head off!" That's just what she'd do if anyone approached her baby.

Minutes later, the baby hurled forth, falling

---

[5]   Gary Richmond, *It's a Jungle Out There* (Eugene, OR: Harvest House Publishers, 1996).

ten feet and landing on its back. Within seconds, it rolled upright with its legs tucked under its body. The mother took a quick look, positioned herself directly over her baby, swung her leg out, and kicked her baby so hard it sent it sprawling head over heels.

Gary was shocked. The baby didn't get up. Mom positioned herself over baby again and kicked it again, repeating the violent process as the baby struggled each time to rise. The mother giraffe never gave up until, amidst cheers from the zoo staff, the baby stood for the first time . . . wobbly and shaking, but on its own.

The mother cared less about affection than safety. She wanted the baby to learn to get up fast. In the wild, it would have needed to get up as soon as possible to follow the herd and avoid being eaten alive by lions, hyenas, or leopards.

Sometimes being "nice" can get others killed. Sometimes rushing in to help can get *you* killed!

Reflections

• What are your particular strengths as a leader?

- Who is a leader that you really admire?
- Could you be a "tough" leader when necessary? Why or why not?

8

Using Your Gifts

I am not afraid of storms for I am learning how to sail the ship.

—Louisa May Alcott, *Little Women*

You don't have to be perfect to lead

The Wild West character Calamity Jane has something to teach us about being a leader. Martha Jane Canary (May 1, 1852 – August 1, 1903) is better known as "Calamity Jane," a noted American frontierswoman and professional scout who was an acquaintance of Wild Bill Hickok. Jane was the eldest of six children. Her father had a gambling problem, and her mother had spent time working as a prostitute.

After her mother died, and she had to help support the family, Martha Jane worked as a dishwasher, cook, waitress, dance hall girl, nurse, and ox team driver. Later she is said to have found work as a scout at Fort Russell. During that time, she also began her on-and-off employment as a prostitute at the Fort Laramie Three-Mile Hog Ranch. She later moved on to a rougher, mostly outdoor and adventurous life on the Great Plains.

Some accounts claim she married Wild Bill, had a daughter with him, and later when he was killed, she went after his murderer with a meat cleaver! One story reports that she got her nickname because to run up again her was to "court calamity."

Late in her life, she appeared in Buffalo Bill's Wild West Show as a storyteller.

She was noted for being a daredevil.

She was also known for her habit of wearing men's attire.

She exhibited compassion to others, especially to the sick and needy.

She claimed things she witnessed and participated in but couldn't prove.

She was an alcoholic and in later years suffered from depression.

She did not have a formal education.

She sure wasn't a saint.

But by all accounts, she did know how to lead people through dangerous territory and get them safely to their destination. And that is what each of us is called to do—in some way, at certain times—in our relationships.

Your past failures can work for you

You've heard it before: David was an adulterer and murderer, Peter was a coward and betrayer, Mary Magdalene was beset by seven demons . . . and yet they were called by God to partner in his saving work. They, and all the saints with a sinful past, are in some sense better equipped to relate to others.

Do you come from a broken family?

Have you struggled with alcohol, depression, or impure relationships?

Do you have a limited education or a meat-cleaver temper?

If I wanted to travel on a covered wagon to

head West in search of gold, I would probably hire Perfect Poindexter from Princeton with his meticulous manners and many maps. But I would also want Calamity Jane, with her rough language, and scars from Indian arrows and grizzly bear claws. Poindexter knows where to go; she knows where *not* to.

God doesn't call the perfect; he *perfects* the ones he calls. If you waited until all of your issues were conquered to step in and lead others, you'd be waiting a long time. It is precisely through leading, helping, and even appropriately rebuking others that your own sanctification will be completed.

Grace builds on nature. Don't let your character defects and past failures hold you back from allowing God to continue to re-form you. Stand tall, saddle up, and lead others into the kingdom. Your past failures can be redeemed and used by God to help guide others.

You can lead like Jesus

Jesus was a wild man too. He didn't sin, but Jesus sure caused trouble:

He got angry and whipped people out of his Father's temple (see Mt 21:12–23).

He came to set the world on fire (see Lk 12:49).

He said he came to divide families (see Mt 10:35).

He called people out and issued dire warnings. (see Mt 23:27).

He called some names, like "whitewashed tombs filled with dead men's bones" (see Mt 23:27–28).

He infuriated the Pharisees, so much so that they wanted to kill him (see Mt 12:14).

Believe it or not, these are all some of the ways that Jesus was leading people to the Truth. For their own good! This side of Jesus is uncomfortable or even seems unthinkable. Often in relationships we have to be "wild" like Jesus. We have to be so filled with the Spirit of Truth, so confident in our mission and love for others, and so clear in our role in relationships, that we do not fear their slings and arrows. We want what is best for them.

Don't worry; leading like Jesus isn't just about

throwing furniture around. How else did Jesus lead?

He taught by telling stories

Think back to your childhood, adolescence, young adult years, and beyond and recall the funniest, scariest, or most meaningful experiences you've had. What lessons did you learn or what eternal truths do they convey? Instead of telling others that rules are to keep people safe, help them understand more deeply with your own "parable" about driving in Mexico.

He quoted Scripture

Jesus often referred to the Old Testament when he was teaching. The more you read the Bible, the more verses will be building up in your memory, like arrows in your quiver. Not only for the purpose of God leading you, but for using when necessary to lead others.

He led by example

Sometimes the most powerful way of leading is to simply let others see you take the high path yourself. They may be shut down to listening to your wise counsel, but they still see what you do.

He asked questions

It's true that sometimes the answers are inside us; not because *we* are so brilliant, but because God wired us to know his truth when we hear it, especially when our consciences have been well-formed. We may just need someone to help us remember. Learn to ask more and lecture less.

He gave direct commands

Sometimes a non-offensive, drawn out dialogue is an exercise in ego and a waste of time. Depending on the circumstance and the person, Jesus often skipped the stories and Scripture and went right to the heart of the matter. *Go and sin no more* (see Jn 8:11).

He affirmed and encouraged

"Atta girl!" is a strong and beautiful way to lead others to keep going in the way they should go.

He rebuked

We don't like giving or receiving this one. But if someone is about to spiritually wander off into danger or morally ingest poison, love demands that we cry out. Never worry about who will be offended when you speak the hard truths; worry, instead, about who will be misled, deceived, or confused.

He laid his life down in different ways

Jesus said, "Greater love has no man than this, that a man lay down his life for his friends" (Jn 15:13). But he didn't lay his life down when they came to stone him—he slipped away to hide from their harm (see Lk 4:30; see also Jn 6:15). Was he being stingy or cowardly? No, it just wasn't the right time, place, or reason to suffer.

Your role will change

Depending on the person or circumstance, your leadership role will change. You can lead others like Jesus in one or more of these ways; which ones come most easily to you?

- Facilitator – you're unafraid to help steer things back on track
- Teacher – you have important information to share
- Comforter – you use kind words, understanding, and appropriate touches
- Coach – you offer a gentle nudge or exhortation when needed
- Consultant – you coach and guide rather than direct
- Nurse – you keep tissues and cough drops on hand for those who need them
- Guard – you stand up for the rights and dignity of others
- Problem-Solver – you easily come up with perfect solutions
- Mediator – you help mediate any disagreements if necessary

- Bouncer – you're not afraid to get rid of what is inappropriate
- Spiritual director – you see the biggest picture and share it

Know your limits, though. Someone else maybe more experienced or qualified to lead them further. Don't take on responsibility that God did not intend for you to have. There are many others in the world God is using to bring his hope and healing. Maybe this time you are not the one.

Sometimes you will be Veronica

Maybe all we can do is let others know we are here for them and wipe away their blood, sweat, and tears. We can offer encouragement and support and nothing else. But isn't that all that Jesus needed at that moment? It was not Veronica's job to save Jesus. He was saving her.

Sometimes you will be Simon

We can help someone with life's heavy lifting, but often the most loving thing you can do is allow the person to carry their cross and experience some form of crucifixion. Don't worry, your assistance will be valuable. It seems paradoxical, but resurrection, freedom, and new life cannot come but by way of our crosses.

Sometimes you will be Mary

When you feel powerless and know that it is not your place to interfere with another's "passion," unite your sorrow with the Mother of Sorrows. Our Blessed Mother walked with her Son along the Via Dolorosa and watched him fall three times. She knew this horror was necessary, and she trusted God, *but she still grieved.* Ask her to stand with you and weep.

Reflections

- Where do your leadership skills shine brightest? At home, school, work?
- Are you more a teacher or a mediator?
- Are you mostly Simon or Veronica?

9

Letting Them Fall

Therefore, I will hedge up her way with
thorns; and I will build a wall against her,
so that she cannot find her paths.

—Hosea 2:6

A little girl playing in her back yard discovered a beautiful caterpillar. She carefully picked it up and brought it inside to show her mom. Mother helped her make a comfy home for the creature inside a glass mason jar where they put some green leaves and a little stick so the caterpillar could climb it and wouldn't get bored. Funny how children—and some of us adults—are terrified of boredom!

A few weeks later, the girl noticed that the

caterpillar, which she had named Wiggles, was acting strangely.

"Mom, come look!"

Her mother explained that Wiggles was making a cocoon and was going through metamorphosis and was to soon become a butterfly.

"Wow!" exclaimed the little girl. She imagined how beautiful the butterfly would be and just could not wait to see it happen.

The next day, she saw that Wiggles was covered in a gauzy white material, and by the end of the second day, her caterpillar had completely disappeared into the cocoon. Every day the girl checked to see if the butterfly had appeared, and after a few weeks, she started to grow impatient.

Sometimes helping hurts

One morning, she noticed movement within the cocoon and ran to tell her mother.

"Mom! Wiggles is moving! What's happening in there? The butterfly is coming!"

The girl jumped up and down and twirled a few times with happiness.

"Well honey, not yet," said Mother. "Wiggles

has to still struggle a bit before she can come out. We'll have to wait some more." Mother went back to the kitchen.

All day long the girl worried about Wiggles. *Struggle?* She loved her little butterfly and didn't want her to struggle. *Maybe I can help*, thought the girl.

She ran into her room, got out her scissors, and went to the mason jar. Careful not to hurt Wiggles, she gently snipped a tiny end of the cocoon. She looked more closely and could see part of the new black and orang wing inside! Then she slowly worked at the hole to make it bigger until Wiggles squirmed and eventually crawled out.

But something looked wrong. The butterfly's body was swollen, and the wings were small and shriveled. She waited for them to get bigger and for Wiggles to fly.

But nothing happened.

Wiggles just crawled around on the bottom of the jar—fat, wet, and forever unable to fly.

"Oh, honey," Mother said when the girl ran crying to her arms. "I know you meant to help, but Wiggles needed to struggle. The struggle releases the fluids that would make her too heavy to fly. Just like your muscles, her wings could only get big and strong by exercising them."

I first learned about "enabling" when my sister and I attended an AL-Anon 12-Step meeting after realizing there was alcoholism in our family. I had always thought my role in relationships was to help—especially growing up as the oldest of nine children. And especially as a Christian. That's what we do, relieve others of their suffering, right? Not when it relieves them of an important opportunity to learn and grow.

Sometimes hurting helps

"But *Dad*, admit it; MOM IS A @#$%!"

I was in high school, complaining to my father about what a pain my mother was and feeling far too big for my britches. I had been arguing with Mom and she'd told Dad. Then Dad came downstairs to talk to me.

In a way, I shocked myself that those words had just left my brain and actually came out of my mouth. I had let an F-bomb fly in front of my father for the first time! But there, I said it.

I was angry at Mom, feeling righteous in my indignation, and I knew Dad would understand. I'd heard him upset with Mom too.

But I wasn't prepared for what happened next.

The look on Dad's face changed to one I had never seen before—or afterwards—*and he slapped me hard across the face.* So hard I stumbled backwards.

I was SHOCKED! I put my hand up against my burning cheek and cowered timidly as he got in my face and carefully, calmly, but with great authority said the words I will never forget:

"Don't you EVER talk about my wife like that again."

My wife. I had never heard him refer to Mom like that in front of me. I burst into tears as he walked back upstairs. I was surprised at the mixture of emotions that flooded in after that: I was ashamed, humbled . . . and intrigued.

- I had just witnessed how deeply my father loved my mother. That made me feel secure.
- I had just seen a real man stand up for his wife, placing her appropriately above the children. Not many husbands will do that.

I remember thinking *I want to marry a man like that!* A man who protects, defends, and respects me so much even his own beloved children cannot manipulate, connive, convince, or otherwise turn him away from what is due his wife. She comes first.

- I had just experienced my father rebuke me in love. It hurt my pride but made me feel loved. He risked offending me to knock me off my high horse and back to a place of humility and gratitude. That didn't make me resent him; it made me want to live up to his standards.

Was it physical abuse? You can argue, but at that point, my pride was so stiff-necked that I needed a serious reprimand. When the heart is hard, sometimes words are not enough. The result for me was sorrow, repentance, and a desire to be good.

False compassion is not loving

Bishop Fulton J. Sheen—whom I grew up watching on television—often spoke on "false compassion." This is where we feel excessively sorry for others, focusing on the positive good that can be found in every person or situation, but excluding the negative. He referred to those who prided themselves on this false compassion as "social slobberers," since they cried over the poor harshly convicted drug dealer, rapist, or abortionist. After all, perpetrators have rights and feelings too.

We do not lead others into the truth when we live with them in the lies. False compassion blinds us to the greater good and is fed by our feeling virtuous. We buy our children the things their father said no to; we overlook laziness, selfishness, and disrespect because it doesn't seem that bad. We tolerate sexual sin and even perversion because we love the person and don't want to make them feel bad or lose their affection. We are purchasing a false peace at the cost of truth, and we leave others unable to fly, or worse, crawling along in life with a bloated ego.

Don't let self-love get in the way of true love.

Unbridled compassion is a counterfeit love

In the last few decades, we have ruled our relationships primarily by feelings, not the true faith. Even good Catholics have reinvented Christianity by taking Jesus off the cross and remaking him into a softer, gentler teacher and friend. We ignore or reject the side of Jesus that ruffled feathers, publicly chastised church leaders, and called his friend "Satan"(see Mt 16:23). When we don't want to see who he really is, either from fear or arrogance or both, we mere creatures attempt to co-opt the Almighty God to suit our agenda.

But this modern Jesus, who loves and tolerates everyone and everything, is a hideous counterfeit who peddles relationship destruction. Beauty without truth, charity without discipline, and tenderness without toughness all lead to moral and spiritual corruption and death. And as we continue to wallow in our emotions and celebrate all manner of relationship sin, we even bring physical death upon ourselves.

I am continually struck by the piercing quote from Catholic novelist Flannery O'Connor

(1925–1964): "If other ages felt less, they saw more, even though they saw with the blind, prophetical, unsentimental eye of acceptance, which is to say, of faith. In the absence of this faith now, we govern by tenderness. It is a tenderness which, long cut off from the person of Christ, is wrapped in theory. When tenderness is detached from the source of tenderness, its logical outcome is terror. It ends in forced-labor camps and in the fumes of the gas chamber."[6]

When we allow those we love to stay in their addictions, sexual immoralities, or wickedness of heart, we are passively leading them to the gas chamber of their own sinfulness. It's a paradox of our faith: the true "source of tenderness" is the bloody, splintery cross by which Our Lord showed his greatest compassion, tenderness, and love in suffering for our greater good.

We must expect suffering in relationships.

We must be willing to endure it ourselves.

We must courageously lead others to truth.

---

[6]   Flannery O'Connor, *Mystery and Manners: Occasional Prose* (New York, NY: Farrar, Straus, and Giroux, 1969).

We must allow others to suffer the consequences of their own actions.

If we can't accept these things, *we are not capable of love.*

Reflections

- Do you see yourself as compassionate? Why or why not?
- Have you ever had false compassion for someone?
- Has some leader (parent, teacher, boss, pastor) ever been too harsh with you?

PART 4

Loving

True love does not demand a re-
ward, but it deserves one.

—Bernard of Clairvaux, *On Loving God*

10

Being a Gift

*Your words should be like gifts, like lit-
tle silver boxes with bows on top.*

—Florence Littauer, *Silver Boxes*

When I was a kid, Dad would call all of
us children into the living room on Sunday after Mass and hand out our allowance. The
older kids got a dollar, and the younger ones a
handful of change. Barb and I—the two oldest—would immediately hop on our bikes and
ride off to the grocery store where we'd shop for
comic books and candy bars.

Back then, *Superman, Archie,* and other com-
ics were ten cents each and so were candy bars.
For only a dollar, we could get a ton of good
stuff! Then we'd ride home, go into my bedroom,

and spread out all our treasures on the bed. Sometimes we'd split a candy bar, sometimes we traded. We read for hours and stuffed our faces. It was heaven.

One day, I overheard a troubling conversation between two of my younger brothers.

"Joe, why don't you give me your dime? I'll give you my nickel since it's bigger!"

My brother Charlie was good at seductive bargaining with Joe, who was one year younger.

"Okay, Charlie!" said four-year-old Joe, beaming and happy that Charlie was being so generous with him.

"NO, JOE! Don't do it! Charlie is tricking you!" I hollered.

"Ha-ha, *just kidding*, Joe!" devious Charlie would say.

Joe was—and still is—kind, thoughtful, sweet, and unmeasured in his love for others. He usually followed Charlie around and wanted to be like him. Charlie often took advantage of that.

Another time, I discovered that Charlie had talked Joe into giving him all of his candy.

"Where's your candy, Joe?" I asked.

"I gave it to Charlie."

"*What?* Why?"

"He wanted it."

I rolled my eyes.

"Joe, it's good to share but you didn't have to give him everything!"

I'll never forget Joe's reply or the sweet, sincere look on Joe's face.

"It's okay, Rosie. *I wanted to.*"

Self-love blocks abundant love

Authentic love never reduces a person to an object to be used. Charlie had turned his brother into a vending machine who should dispense the goodies upon demand. On the contrary, authentic love is generous, poured out without measure even to complete emptiness. If a person who says they love you is not willing to sacrifice, *it's not love.* It's trading, bartering, negotiating. It's business.

St. John of the Cross was a sixteenth-century Carmelite and mystic. He's a master of the interior life and known for his passionate teachings about conquering "inordinate attachments" to the good things of this world so that we can sur-render to God's love. Only then can we be filled with it to the extent it pours out on others. What does he say is the only thing that prevents us from loving God and others as we should?

Self-love.

Not the healthy self-respect that reverences all that is good in us and appropriately cares for our genuine well-being as St. Paul tell us: "For no man ever hates his own flesh, but nourishes and cherishes it, as Christ does the church" (Eph 5:29).

It's not necessarily sinful self-love to playfully post "selfies" on social media or feel excited, proud, and happy about our accomplishments. Those can all be good things. Rather, it's the self-focus that blocks unmeasured love to others, a holding back to ensure our own comfort, secu-rity, or pleasure first. It offers half of a candy bar, maybe even the biggest piece, but is reluctant to hand over the whole cache.

In your own adventure into the interior, I pray that you will allow God to lead you out of well-disguised spiritual narcissism. When we are yet immature in our spiritual life—no matter our physical age—God will give us sweets to help us to love and trust him. But he created us for much greater gifts, and eventually he desires that we put away childish things (see 1 Cor 13:11) to learn to love as he does.

Love can be a simple touch

A simple act can mean extravagant love. I was deeply moved when I once watched a documentary about Mother Teresa and her missionaries.

With veils pinned back and sleeves rolled up, the sisters scurried busily about the hospital ward tending to various the medical needs of the sick children. One emaciated, brown-skinned boy lay curled in a fetal position in a whitewashed crib when the slender sister approached him. While his eyes stared blankly into space, she bent down toward him, scooped her arm beneath his head, and lifted him slightly.

At being moved and feeling her touch, his eyes darted furtively, and like a frightened animal, he began to twitch nervously. I watched to see if she was going to feed him or give him medicine or some other medical treatment. What she gave him surprised me.

The young nurse simply began to rub the boy's chest with firm circular strokes. She broadened her strokes to include his shoulders and neck, and back down around his heart. Her capable hands moved up over his face, around his scalp and neck, and back down to his chest. Quietly and faithfully she worked her repetitive touch on his frail body.

Slowly, his twitching eased, his body relaxed, and his darting eyes moved to her face and stayed there. As his eyes locked on hers, I saw the connection between them and the powerful healing of physical touch. Breaking his isolation and loneliness, the young woman's loving hands brought the patient from panic to peace.

Sometimes the best way to *love* someone— whether they have *listened* to you, allowed you to *lead* them or not—is to simply offer them a loving touch anyway.

Pat your kids on the back or their head. Hug your friends. Hold hands with your elderly neighbor, kiss your parents on the lips. And if

you need some healthy human touch, get a man-
icure or, better yet, a mani-pedi!

Love is meant to be extravagant

I speak and write a lot about my father. We
were of the same take-charge temperament and
shared a common outlook on life. I worked with
him for thirty years in the family business and
still miss him. But what about my mother?

Mom was beautiful, smart, highly educated,
and deeply devoted to the faith, but she and I
bumped heads for decades. Where she was calm
and of good Midwest stock, I was a wild California girl. She was an introvert; I am an extrovert.
Where she would have preferred me to listen
more, in my childish arrogance, I often chal-
lenged her head-on. We did love each other, and
in later years came to terms, but many times it
wasn't pretty.

In my twenties, as I was trying to find my way
in the world, she let me know that she favored
my sisters over me. She would invite them all to
lunch, but not me. She would give some of her

jewelry to them, but none for me. I tried to let it roll off my back, but it hurt.

One chilly Saturday morning in late November, I drove over to my sister Malia's house (this was decades before Armani) for coffee. Her children, Raymond and Lisa, played in the next room while Malia put the coffee percolator on the stove. I went to her cupboard to find cups—and my hurt and anger all came bubbling over.

But I need to back up.

When we were children, every December a huge Christmas package would arrive at our home from Grandma Riley in Kansas City, MO. I recall one year while the younger children were napping, Mom let me help her open the box, which this particular year seemed much bigger than ever. Inside we found lots of tagged presents, the usual decorative tin with Grandma's homemade fruitcake[7] inside, and—surprise!—a full service for twelve of beautiful, delicate bone china, hand-painted with red and green Christmas holly and gold edging. It was gorgeous!

We'd never used good place settings; with all

---

[7]   You can find the recipe here https://rosesweet.com/christmas-fruitcake/.

those kids, it had to be unbreakable Melmac. Mom let me set the table for Christmas dinner, and every year after that, it became our family tradition that I would be the one to carefully pull out the Christmas china and set an exquisite table.

Now, Grandma's name was Rosemary, my mother's name was Rosemary, and my given name is also Rosemary. Since I was the oldest daughter—and Grandma's namesake—I *knew* that someday I would get those dishes. I deserved those dishes! I needed those dishes!

But that Saturday morning, I saw them in Malia's cupboard.

"Why are THESE dishes HERE?" I demanded.

I couldn't believe it. Of all the low-handed, slap-in-the face moves Mom could have done.

"Whoa, what is going on?" Malia asked.

I realized she didn't know. Malia is our baby sister and was probably never aware of how much I loved Grandma's china, so I told her the whole story and then tried to calm down. After all, they were *just* dishes.

"Well, I'm sorry . . . I don't know why Mom

gave them to me, but I was happy she did. To tell you the truth, I always loved those dishes too, Rose. It's probably because of how beautiful *you* made the table look every year when I was little."

That did make me feel a little better.

The next Saturday, my doorbell rang, and I saw Malia outside with her kids and three large, new Macy's shopping bags. I knew immediately she had bought me my own beautiful set of Christmas china, and my heart swelled with love and gratitude for her.

But I was wrong.

The bags contained Grandma's delicate dishes—all twelve place settings.

Macy's china would have been sisterly love; Grandma's china was sweet, sacrificial, saintly love. Love *extravagantly*. The broken world awaits you.

Reflections

- When has someone been stingy with you?
- When have you been stingy with attention, praise, or love with others?
- When has someone been extra-generous toward you?

11

Adjusting Your Expectations

*The definition of insanity is doing the same
thing over and over and expecting different results.*

—widely credited to Albert Einstein

Loving others can mean a long wait

When I was small, I longed for my mother's hugs and kisses. She was kind and gentle but wasn't the touchy-feely type with anyone. Except for one vivid memory I have as a five-year-old. I was feeling very grown up now that I was in kindergarten; every day was an adventure of monkey bars, alphabet songs, and recess games. But when I came home one afternoon, all my younger siblings were down for a nap and drinking bottles. Mom was tucking them in and fluffing their covers.

"Mom?" I asked timidly. "Can I have a bottle too?"

I remember thinking how silly that was since I was such a big girl now. I expected Mom to laugh and tell me I was too grown up for all that now, but she didn't.

"Sure, honey. I'll put some Ovaltine in it."

Ovaltine! My favorite.

I laid on my bed and Mom handed me a bottle. I felt so conflicted sucking on the rubber nipple but, boy, the chocolate milk tasted so good!

Then, instead of leaving me to sleep, she sat down on the edge of my bed, looked at me tenderly, and began to gently stroke my hair away from my forehead.

She didn't say a word, but she spoke love to me with her hands and I soon drifted off to sleep.

That's my last memory of Mom showing me any physical affection.

My mother was also not the type to hand out praise without good cause. She was a perfectionist, and I was definitely not perfect. Deep down I knew she loved me, but it was hard for her to say it and hard for me not hear it very often. I did merit a few measured praises from her when I helped around the house. By the time I was seven or eight, I was able to cook the family breakfast, fix school lunches, make beds, sort the laundry, and take care of the crying babies. I loved being in charge!

When I did these things, Mom would show me occasional kindness in her tone of voice and a gentle smile. But I don't recall her praising me for much of anything else except for an occasional good report card. She was highly educated and would often correct me with a long lecture about how I didn't really know or understand. She was absolutely right, but I was absolutely crushed.

Forget being smart or helpful around the house; what I really wanted was to be beautiful like Mom and for her to tell *me* I was pretty. Mom was a striking redhead with pale Irish-cream skin and delicate features, and she'd had modeling jobs when she was in her twenties. Like some mothers, I think she feared that if she were too generous in her compliments, it might make me vain. So, to save me from myself, she kept her mouth shut most of her life. And I kept waiting for a word—any word—of praise.

In the 1940s, she'd been the first female chemist for Transworld Airlines (TWA) and had worked for Howard Hughes, the famous aviator, industrialist, film producer and director, and one of the wealthiest people in the world. Mom had a brilliant mind and could have soared in a career, but she ended up at home with all of us kids. She'd probably always felt that nobody ever really understood or appreciated her. I know she loved us the best she could, and I value the many things she taught us, but until her dying day, she refused to let anyone very far into her guarded heart.

A few years before she died, she succumbed to dementia and hardly recognized or spoke to anyone when they came to visit. Although frustrating, it was also a relief because Mom lost that hard, protective wall that she'd always maintained. I used to visit her in the nursing home and bring her favorite browned-butter cookies. Week after week, we'd sit in silence while she ate the treats and stared off into some faraway place. One day, however, while I was sitting with her on her patio, she turned and looked straight at me. Her eyes were clear and bright, and she studied me with a slightly cocked head and a growing smile on her face.

"You're very pretty!" she observed.

I was stunned!

And then, as quickly as the smile had come, it was gone, and again she stared blankly into the distance.

Not only had she spoken, but those were the words I had longed to hear from her for most of my life! And yet when she finally said them, they didn't mean nearly as much as I thought they would.

Immediately, I realized two things: one, that those words had been there all the time; she just couldn't say them. And, two, that as long as I stayed focused on what I couldn't get from her, I'd never be able to love her as she needed.

I said quietly, "Thanks, Mom," touched her hand, and then I thanked God that somehow with the dementia came an unlocking of her heart. Mom died in 2003, but I treasure that moment on her patio. I *was* pretty, and she was finally free to tell me so.

Loving others means changing the dance

All those years of fruitless, pointless fighting with my mother. Whatever you are doing in a relationship that is not working—including futile arguments—stop it! Most of the time, someone's ears are closed by fear (of being controlled, of losing, etc.). If for whatever reason they can't be reasonable, why are you still arguing with them?

Part of arguing is defensiveness, a natural ego-driven need to be heard. But we can get carried away and spend far too much time "dextifying:" *defending, explaining, and testifying*. More exhaustion!

My spiritual director is a wise priest who recalls the time his father called him and his younger brother into his room

"Sons, I'm going to tell you the secret to a good marriage: *she's right!*" As teens, they both rolled their eyes, but the younger brother has had a long and happy marriage of not arguing with his wife because *she's right*. Father quipped to me, "I use that advice with my bishop!"

It doesn't feel good or natural to let go, but when someone can't or won't listen or stop disrespecting you, get off the dance floor. Your emotional "feet" will thank you!

- You may not be able to change or fix someone who has deep-seeded relationship problems, but you can change your own response to them.
- You can change your outlook and your attitude.
- You can stop expecting people with problems to make you happy.
- You can stop making your spouse, children, friends, and even the people to whom you minister at work or Church, your primary source of happiness.

Loving others might mean rearranging the furniture.

"What am I going to do Rose? I can't divorce him, but I can't go on the way things have been." The woman in my office burst into tears. After a year of couples' counseling, the therapist advised that her husband still blamed everything on her and he was likely never going to change. I've been in similar situations in relationships and knew what to tell her.

I call it rearranging the furniture.

I get excited with make-overs, remodels, and home decorating. Say you need a change, but moving or buying new furniture is out of the question. Then repurpose or rearrange what you have and—voila!—a new home! Sometimes in relationships, we should do the same thing.

- You don't change your husband, but you can change other things: the patterns, responses, routines, even physical space. You can create a new "design" for the way you live out a difficult marriage. Still holy, still loving, but different.

- You don't disown your children, but you can change the way you respond to them. New rules, new consequences, different day-to-day dynamics.

- You don't end the forty-year friendship with your girlfriend, but you start to do it a bit differently. You don't quit your job, but you quit the old patterns.

Here are some "designer" ideas!

(1) Stop expecting the old to fit in the new.

All that does it set you up to remain angry and bitter. Most anger comes from unmet expectations, so change the expectations. Who else can help you clean the house or carry the load at work? Rethink your routines. Nothing changes if nothing changes.

(2) Be creative—move things around.

Your husband snores? Don't tolerate something that drives you crazy. Find another place, time, or way to work around it. Ear plugs are good, a separate room may be better! Think outside the box. Be daring. Keep what is good and get rid of what is not.

(3) Don't feel guilty

As long as you are not breaking a commandment, you have a lot of freedom in making your life work for you and pleasing to the Lord at the same time. A happier and freer you will be able to love others more.

One woman I counseled was in therapy with her husband but still feeling high anxiety and even entertaining divorce. They had serious problems to work out, but in the meantime, she was also feeling hopeless and trapped in her home, with no place to go for privacy or peace. Instead of shipping her children off forever to boarding school or murdering her husband, I suggested the two kids share a room and she take over one of their rooms to create a small retreat for herself. She was shocked!

"But don't my children need a bedroom of their own?"

"No, they do not."

"But isn't that selfish?"

"If this keeps you from divorce or murder, it's not selfish!"

We both laughed.

You don't have to suffer endlessly or needlessly. You don't have to consider extreme measures to fix a lot of common relationship problems. Sometimes they are huge and there are no quick or clever fixes. Just as you would pay a doctor, dentist, auto mechanic, or beautician, get professional help if you need it.

Reflections

- In what relationship have you held unrealistic expectations?
- Have you ever kept a relationship but changed the dance?
- What change could you make today to improve a relationship?

12

Respecting Their Freedom

Freedom consists not in doing what we like, but
in having the right to do what we ought.

—St. John Paul II, Homily at Camden Yards, Baltimore, 1995

"Mom, why doesn't Dad even care about us?"

Carla reminded her son, Mark, that his father had abandoned them when he was ten. But now that he was thirteen, he was hoping his mother would open up and share more about his dad.

"Well, honey, I've told you this answer before. He's a self-centered, lying creep," his mother replied sarcastically.

For the next decade, his mother's constant trash-talk about his father made Mark believe maybe his father *was* a total jerk. After high school graduation, Mark decided to enlist in the Navy. At the recruiter's office, an officer asked about his father.

"I don't know where my father is, and frankly, I don't care."

The man set his face and responded.

"Son, I don't know your background or what happened, but I'll tell you one thing: you need to find your dad and make some kind of contact with him. I don't know how it will turn out for you, but if you don't at least make the effort, it will eat away at you for life. A man takes care of unfinished business."

Mark didn't know what to say but nodded quietly, and over the next few weeks, the old desire to see and know his father worked its way back into his heart. Mark started searching on the internet, and after a few days, he found his father. When he told his mom, the years of resentment erupted, and she threw her coffee cup at him. He ducked as it shattered on the wall behind him.

"*Get out.* Go join the damn Navy. I don't

care what happens to your father or you! GET OUT!"

Love doesn't fear freedom

It's rare that we ever really know someone's whole story. It's easier, quicker, or can satisfy our egos to accept what we see on the surface. Sometimes we simply trust what someone we love has told us about another. I've learned the hard way not to judge without all the facts, and in this life, we may never have them all.

Mark is not his real name, and some of the conversation here is fictional but typical of separated families. Do you want to hear the rest of this true story?

Mark's mother and father, Jim, had married young and in haste. When the marriage ended, his dad spent his life savings in long and costly court battles. But his ex-wife's family had more money and more legal clout. When Carla took Mark to hide out of state, his father ran out of money, got depressed, and gave up for the interim.

"I wasn't the perfect husband and father, but I

was trying," Jim shared with me. "I didn't know what else to do. For years I sent my child support and insurance payments to her attorney, but I had no idea where my son was. Or what he even looked like."

It wasn't just Jim who grieved. For years, Mark's grandparents and other extended family and friends mourned the loss of their young family member.

The first few phone calls between Mark and his dad were guarded and short, but they finally agreed to meet face-to-face and spent hours listening, talking, and rediscovering the love they had for one another. When it was time to leave, they hugged and planned to get together again soon.

"Dad, can you just remember you don't *really* know me?" Mark stated carefully.

"I know, son, but I plan to rectify that in short order!"

Jim called Mark on the way home with an idea about reuniting the whole family at Christmas. What a tearful and joyful reunion it was! Grandparents, cousins, and friends all gathered to welcome Mark back into that side of his family.

Sadly, his mother could not ever forgive Jim. She rejected any invitations by the family and felt betrayed that her son had "gone over to the other side." Two years later, when Mark met a wonderful young woman and invited his whole family to the wedding, his father and others on that side of the family joyfully attended.

His mother did not attend.

Regardless of the details, this story is too common in a divorce-ridden culture. I stand behind any parent who needs to protect his or her child from the other parent who may be abusive and even dangerous. But in many cases, it is not abuse but hurt, pride, and fear that keeps us enslaved.

As Mark grew up, he should have been free to talk about and reach out to his father. Depending on his age and the circumstance, if Carla wanted to caution, prepare, or guide him in the process, she could have.

Too often we can use our children or others to manipulate a satisfying outcome. We hover and become "helicopter parents" or, worse, "smother mothers." In doing so, we disregard the child's dignity and freedom. That's not love, it's fear. We can be controlling in any kind of relationship when we are afraid we might lose something we really want. Even when what we desire is good, we can be too emotionally attached to that desire. We must be careful that our fears do not keep us from denying another's freedoms.

Scripture tells us that perfect love casts out fear (see 1 Jn 4:18). Think about that for a moment; it's knowing and remembering *God's perfect love* that will cast out the excess fear you have in other relationships.

Love is letting go of fear

Her wedding day was fast approaching, and nothing could dampen Jennifer's excitement, not even her parents' recent nasty divorce. After a long but fun day of shopping, her mother finally found the perfect dress for the event and would be the best-dressed mother of the bride ever!

A week later, Jennifer was horrified to discover her new, young stepmother, Barbie, had purchased the same dress. Worried that her mom would be upset, she asked Barbie to exchange her dress.

"Out of respect for my *mother*, please?"

"Absolutely not! I'm going to wear this dress. I look like a million in it!"

Really? thought Jennifer. *Wow.*

Jennifer told her mother, who thought about it and just shrugged her shoulders.

"Honey, I'm not worried, it's fine. I'll get another dress. After all, it's your day, not ours." She hugged her daughter.

Two weeks later, Jennifer and her mother went shopping again and did find another lovely dress. At lunch, Jennifer asked, "Mom, what are you going to do with the first dress? It was so expensive, and you really don't have anywhere else to wear it."

"Of course, I do," the mother replied with a smile. "I'm wearing it to the rehearsal dinner!"

I love this story. The tension between two competitive women can always be broken when one of them lets go of fear and surrenders her desires for being the best or being in control. God wants us to be free of fear, to be loving, forgiving, and trusting in him. That's what will make us look—and feel—like a million.

Reflections

- Have you ever hovered or smothered in a relationship? Why or why not?
- What scares you about giving someone freedom they want?
- What human relationship are you most fearful of losing and why?

PART 5

Letting Go

Detachment. How hard it is! Oh. To be fastened by nothing but three nails and to have no more feeling in my flesh than the Cross!

—Josemaria Escriva, *The Way*

13

Facing Your Fears

There is no living thing that is not afraid when it faces danger. The true courage is in facing danger when you are afraid, and that kind of courage you have in plenty.

—The Wizard to the Cowardly
Lion, *Wizard of Oz*

Detachment, in the interior life—and in all relationships—is being willing to "lose" in order to win.

Sixty-six-year-old Thomas VanderWoude was a retired Navy pilot and Vietnam veteran who was still in great shape. He coached basketball and soccer at the local school where everyone loved him, and he was known for his generosity with family, friends, and the whole community.

Thomas lived on a large Virginia property where he sometimes worked in the back fields. Often, his twenty-year-old son, Joseph—who had Down Syndrome—would accompany his father and help in his work.

One day, Joseph was nowhere to be seen. Neighbors called frantically for Thomas, who ran to see what was wrong. Joseph had fallen into a large septic tank when the cover had collapsed.

Letting go takes courage

Without thinking, Thomas jumped into the foul pit to save his son who was thrashing, gasping, and overcome with fear. Joseph was big and heavy and not like a small child you can pull to the edge of the pool. All Thomas could do was swim down under the filth, hold his breath, and keep lifting his son's head above the sewage so that Joseph could breathe.

By the time two men finally pulled Thomas out of the tank, he had been submerged in the muck for as long as twenty minutes. He was pronounced dead at the hospital. Joseph was in critical condition as he fought infection for several days but eventually recovered.

People in the community were devasted. Thomas was a devout Catholic who attended daily Mass and tried to love others as Jesus loves—with a willingness to *let go* even of his own life so that others could live.

Letting go can feel worse than death

A ninety-year-old woman in Evanston, Illinois lived in a block of charming historic homes and close-knit neighbors. Despite her age, she was alert and aware, well-liked, and enjoyed gardening, often sharing her plants with neighbors. But in 2008, police were called to her home and discovered she had been living with the dead bodies of her three siblings, one of whom had been dead over twenty years!

Apparently the four had lived together and the three had each died of natural causes. One of the local residents reported that she explained away the siblings' absence by telling neighbors that the brother had gone to live with other relatives and that one of her sisters was agoraphobic.

She just couldn't let go—even after death. She was terrified of being alone.

I kept that newspaper clipping for years and then found another like it.

Jean Stevens was a ninety-one-year-old widow who lived in a tumble-down house on a desolate country road, but she didn't live alone. Jean had had the embalmed corpses of her husband and twin sister dug up and, for more than a decade, tended to their remains the best she could until police were tipped off.

She kept her sister, who was dressed in her "best housecoat," on an old couch in the spare room. Jean sprayed the corpse with her sister's favorite perfume. She would put glasses on her and "fix up her face."

Her husband was relegated to a couch in the detached garage.

The woman admitted that part of her worries was that there was nothing after death. How blessed we are in our faith that we know the truth.

These sad and macabre stories illustrate the extremes to which people will go to cling desperately to relationships. Normal loving attachment and grief aside, we *can* get too attached to others.

Some relationships with the living are already "near death" and we still can't let go. We even prop people up in our lives and make the relationship look presentable from the outside. Truly, some relationships need to die, have a funeral, and be buried. Trust me, a bad relationship will make you feel more alone than being single or alone ever will!

Losing can be a way to win

"Mayday! Mayday!"

The legendary Bermuda Triangle, also known as the Devil's Triangle or Hurricane Alley, has been the subject of some mesmerizing magazine articles and some pretty cheesy sci-fi movies. Regardless, it's an interesting visual for what happens when three people are entangled in an issue that properly or ultimately belongs directly between the two.

"Triangulation" is a manipulation tactic where one person will not communicate directly with another person, instead using a third person to relay communication to the second, thus forming a triangle. It's different from simply helping someone.

And usually it's all based in fear.

In extreme cases, the roles are seen as: *Victim, Persecutor, Rescuer*.

Sometimes the persecutor is not a person but a difficult circumstance (divorce) or condition (bankruptcy). Still, people need to find a balance between getting help and dealing directly with their problem. Do you know someone who is always the victim? Do you know someone who always likes to rescue? They always find each other. Too often, they marry.

In relationship triangles, the rescuer needs to step out of the triangle and let go! Some examples in simple, day-to-day relationship interactions:

> (1) Matthew makes a request for money from Daddy, but when Daddy says no, Matthew creates a triangle by bringing in Rescuer Mommy. If Mommy is smart, she will back Dad up and pull herself back out, directing Matthew back to Daddy. In the interim—of course—she

may have to rebuke or teach Matthew, but she knows the distraction, disrespect, and disaster than can happen in this kind of triangle.

(2) Janine is the general manager of a grocery store but isn't very good with interpersonal conflict. She asks Pablo, her produce section manager (who is outgoing and good with people) to tell Hilda, the sometimes-testy dairy crew manager, to keep her section cleaner. Last time something like this happened, Pablo learned the hard way that peers would eventually resent him and continue to disrespect Janine. If Pablo is smart, he will refuse the rescue role, remind Janine that it is *her* job but, as a friend, give her some tips on how to best communicate the admonition.

(3) Kevin thinks his twenty-three-year-old son needs to date a better type of girlfriend and stop sleeping with the one he has. "You need to have a talk with him," he told his wife. "No, honey, *you* need

to have that talk with him." If Kevin's wife is smart, she will help him identify his fears of talking to his son, give him some pointers, and back him up. If Mom always does "the talking," she is not really helping. Instead, as rescuer, she helps to rob both of them of the fruits of a strong and healthy father-son relationship.

It's not always good to do something for someone else when they can and should be doing it themselves.

But not all triangles are bad. Sometimes we need a third party's appropriate help, there being a time to step in and help, but a time to step out (see Eccl 3:6).

God's triangles appropriately assist a relationship

They make things clear, without depriving anyone of their rights or relieving them of their responsibilities. Counselors, judges, mediators, therapists, spiritual directors, parents, friends, and teachers are those who understand their role as an assistant, coach, or advisor. They may step in to assist, but—for their good and the good of all—they eventually step back out, like Simon and Veronica.

The devil's triangles improperly replace a role in a relationship

They do not bring people together but keep them from direct interaction. This kind of rescue is triggered by the rescuer's shortsighted need for feeling valuable and appreciated. The reason we don't recognize these triangles or fall into them so easily is because they look and sound a lot like a God triangle. We're only helping, fixing, and loving, when in reality, we are also intruding.

Any time you see yourself in a "devils triangle," let go and pull out. But to do this you have to know the wisdom—and love—of allowing others to struggle out of their cocoon, to be kicked hard so they can run to safety, or to carry the cross that will save them.

Reflections

- Have you ever stayed in a relationship too long? Why?

- Have you ever been in a relationship triangle? Which role did you have?
- What is a courageous action you've taken in a relationship?

14

Releasing Control

The autumn leaves are here to show
The brilliant beauty of letting go.

—Anonymous

Sometimes life will force you to let go

It was an early morning in 1963 when my brother Charlie, my sister Barb, and I threw on our jeans, wolfed down some Rice Krispies, and hopped on our Schwinn bicycles. We pedaled down the street, past the cemetery, and into the almond orchard where, in the spring, the trees had been bursting with pink and white blossoms and looked like a field of cotton candy.

That summer day, though, the trees were green and full of fruit.

We spotted Mr. Parker in his old Chevy pickup truck. He was our neighbor, a quiet man with big biceps and a Navy tattoo, and he invited us to help him harvest almonds. We watched as he unrolled and shook out a large tarp and laid it down under one slender tree whose branches hung heavy with nuts. Then, much to my horror and surprise, Mr. Parker pulled out the biggest sledgehammer I think I've ever seen, told us to step back, and gave the tree a mighty whack!

The tree shook from top to bottom, and in an instant, it was raining hundreds of nuts, every branch giving up its fruit. Mr. Parker threw us each a gunnysack, and we scrambled on all fours to gather up the almonds. When I crawled close to see where Mr. Parker had whacked the tree, there was no visible sign of any damage to the trunk, and the tree stood tall and apparently unharmed.

God doesn't usually directly plan all of the things in life that whack at us; sometimes they are the natural result of our own (or someone else's) poor choices, but he does permit them.

He knows that sometimes we need a crisis to knock us to our senses or to help us let go. With grace, the pain will ease. Our egos may take a blow, but there will be no permanent damage to the soul.

You must not let go of your hopes, dreams, or caring for others, or for your desires for their greatest good. But you should let go of:

- over-involvement,
- overattachment,
- bitterness
- jealousy or envy,
- habitual arguing,
- cold shoulders and silent treatments,
- arrogance and pride,
- anxiety and excess worry,
- self-pity,
- rage,
- naïve or mythical thinking,
- self-centeredness,
- entitlement,
- people who constantly use or abuse you,
- people who continually disrespect you,
- people who deliberately hurt you,

- your right to justice,
- your need for revenge,
- you right to be heard,
- your right to be understood,
- your right to be valued,
- and everything that hinders us from love (see Heb 12:1).

Letting go is not the end

One of my favorite movies is *Castaway*, a survival drama starring Tom Hanks as Chuck, a FedEx employee stranded on an uninhabited island after his plane crashes in the South Pacific. In a devastating scene, he is suddenly sucked out of the aircraft, hurled into the dark, freezing water, and dumped almost lifeless on a deserted beach.

For the majority of the movie, he is the only character, and there is little to no dialogue as we watch his desperate and painful attempts to survive on the island using remnants of his plane's cargo.

Four years later, Chuck has survived despite the island's sparse living conditions. He has become lean and strong, learned to spearfish, collect fresh rainwater, and make fire. But he has been terribly lonely.

A volleyball that had been washed up with Chuck becomes an unlikely companion; in an act of frustration at cutting his hand, Chuck picks up the ball and hurls it into the nearby foliage. Later, he sees that his bloody handprint had made a sort of face on the ball, and he begins to talk to it, naming the ball "Wilson" after the Wilson Sporting Goods manufacturer. During the day, he opens up to, vents, laughs, cries—and bonds—with Wilson. Many nights he sits in silence with the ball by the fire.

Chuck eventually builds a raft and tries to make his way to civilization, and he packs up his provisions and brings his beloved Wilson with him. But our castaway must overcome the barrier reef, a powerful surf, and unmercifully rough waters. A storm nearly tears his raft to pieces, and the next morning, we see Chuck sleeping on the few timbers that are left of the raft. Wilson has become untethered and floated away. Chuck is awakened by the spray of a sounding whale, panics when he sees Wilson out on the waves, and desperately swims after him, calling out, "WILSON! WILSON!"

But Wilson has drifted too far to be safely retrieved, and Chuck nearly drowns in the attempted rescue, realizing Wilson will be lost at sea. Chuck, and we, are devastated.

Chuck makes it back to the raft and collapses in sobs, overwhelmed by loneliness again. As Wilson bobs away farther and farther into the distance, Chuck calls out, "I'm sorry! I'm sorry, Wilson! I'M SORRY."

The movie has a happier ending, but I won't spoil it for you if you haven't seen it. I made some observations about people from the Chuck-Wilson relationship.

- Some people are as emotionally unavailable as volleyballs.
- But when we are afraid to be alone, we will project a loving relationship upon them and bond with them rather than be lonely.
- Even if the relationship is one-sided or otherwise dysfunctional, we grieve terribly when it ends. It's less about the loss of that specific person than the loss of our hopes and

dreams, and our need for communion with others. The tearing of any bond—healthy or not—is painful.

- You can love, forgive, and want the best for another but still move on without them, even when it hurts.

Letting go relieves your pain

No relationship book would be complete without at least briefly addressing codependency. The term may be new to some and seem overused to others. In essence, a codependent person is one who has let another person's behavior adversely affect him or her and who is far too focused with controlling that person's behavior. You could be codependent if you're worried and anxious and have resorted to all sorts of aggressive or passive (or both) behaviors to motivate or change them, even if the changes are for their own good.

If my boyfriend would only___
If my husband would only___
If my child would only_
If my girlfriend would only___
If my boss would only___

If the pope would only___

Regardless, codependency is a modern term for an old Catholic label of being "inordinately attached." Too much weight given to a relationship will tether you to someone who cannot bear that weight. And it will definitely keep you stranded in an ocean of pain.

Just imagine: what kind of women would we be if we could trust God more and worry about controlling others less?

Letting go is a lifetime process

If you humbly and sincerely ask him, God will show you all the little ways you are trying to control. But it may be painful.

Ask my sister Barb, who, after a car accident, had over one hundred stitches in her face. It happened when Barb, nineteen at the time, was missing her fiancé, Art, and decided to do something about it. A little after midnight, she snuck out of the house and drove our family's car along a hypnotizing highway for several hours before she became drowsy, veered off the road, and crashed, landing upside down.

Her face was cut by windshield glass and her nose had been nearly severed, hanging only by a thin piece of skin. A semitruck driver saw it happen from a distance, pulled over, and rushed her to the nearest hospital.

"I was terrified when I saw her bloodied face and the extent of her injuries," he said. "I put her in the front seat of the truck and had her keep talking so she wouldn't lapse into unconsciousness. But when she stopped talking, I told her to sing me a song."

I later asked Barb if she remembered what she had sung.

"'Oh Lord I Am Not Worthy,' our First Holy Communion song."

(Those beautiful prayers and songs we learned from Sister have always been there when we need them.)

When they got to the ER, doctors removed pieces of shattered glass, sewed her nose back on, and held her face together with stitches.

Over the years, Barb reports that every once in a while she will get what she thinks is a blemish on her face but discovers it is a tiny piece of old glass that has worked its way to the surface. Barb doesn't panic; she's learned that with time and patience, her body keeps working to rid itself of what does not belong.

Barb tried to control the situation on her own terms and ended up paying a big price. When our life is shattered by relationship pain, it's likely we will have little shards of fear, worry, and frantic efforts to control just below the surface for a long time. Don't be ashamed when one day you wake up and see once again that fear has worked itself to the surface and you are still trying to control things. Let go, be patient, and trust God's healing process.

Reflections

- Have you ever attached to someone who was emotionally unavailable?
- Have you ever tried to control a relationship with disastrous results?
- Think of someone you know who is controlling. What are they afraid of?

15

Learning to Trust

Trust and trust alone should lead us to love.

—St. Thérèse of Lisieux, *Collected Letters of St. Therese of Lisieux*

The Wicked Witch of the West, in furious pursuit of Dorothy and her companions, flew on her broomstick over the Emerald City to write an ominous demand in the sky: "SUR-RENDER DOROTHY."

Don't do it, Dorothy! I thought when I first watched the movie as a child.

When you surrender, I knew, you lost the good fight. You were weak and the bad guy won. You'd be doomed to imprisonment, torture, or death. For sure you were a coward.

But "surrender" is the very response we must

151

have in our relationship with God. We don't let go of what is good, but we do release what is self-centered. Too many of us fail to progress in the interior life—or in our relationships—because we can't surrender. We are still too busy giving orders!

Peace comes from surrender

Father John Hampsch, a Claretian missionary, called himself an "itinerant preacher-teacher" with a special emphasis on teaching and charismatic healing services, traveling to fifty-eight countries and every state in the United States. With degrees in philosophy and in ascetical and mystical theology, he was also a tenured faculty member in the Pope Leo XIII Institute, training priests in demonology, deliverance, and exorcism. He brought Jesus to millions of people through Catholic and Protestant radio and television.

In the early 1970s, he was in my hometown of Palm Springs, CA where my brother Joe went to hear him speak.

"Father Hampsch had a special talk on peace,"

Joe told me years later. "So, I drove over to St. Theresa's church where he was holding a healing service."

I recall that I'd read some of his books and asked Joe what he remembered about the talk.

"Rose, I will never forget it. He taught that there are two kinds of peace: peace *with* God and the peace *of* God."

"Peace *with* God was won for us by Jesus. He came to make peace between the Father and mankind. If we remain free of mortal sin, we will have that peace *with* God.

But the peace *of* God is different. It is the freedom of inordinate stress and fear. Some people have peace *with* God, but they are still worried and anxious over many things. They do not have the peace *of* God."

Father Hampsh often advised that when one is losing the peace of God, it is helpful to recall God's goodness, his trustworthiness, and that—in a certain sense—nothing on this earth really matters. Everything that is important *is* important but is "nothing" in the eternal picture. The only thing that truly matters is the love of God for each soul and the soul's willingness to surrender to Love.

Joe continued, "Well, Rose, this particular evening he was giving this talk on peace and at the break was looking for some coffee, but they weren't serving any."

"Ugh-h," I complained. "I remember those old church basement affairs where the air conditioning was freezing and there was no coffee *or snacks!*"

We laughed.

"So, he goes poking around and finds the kitchen, but it's all dark. He sees a little red light in the distance and knows it's one of those old plug-in coffee percolators. He fumbles around for a coffee cup, pours some, and drinks it down."

Joe paused dramatically.

"*It was a lye solution.* The cleaning ladies had left it soaking in the pot and had forgotten."

"Oh Lord, Joe!" I could feel my own throat burning just thinking about it.

"They rushed him to Desert Regional Hospital and, as he later tells it, he was lying on the gurney in the ER. He heard the doctor tell a nurse, 'This man has fried his vocal cords. He will never speak again.'"

Panic took over the priest. He realized it was over. His whole ministry was speaking to people all over the world, leading them to Christ. This would end his career; he would be useless. Speaking was what he *did!* Speaking was who he *was!* It was *how* he served the Lord!

As these anxious thoughts raced through his mind and he felt his heart race and tighten into a hard knot, he suddenly remembered his own words.

Joe recalls him sharing that at that moment, he took a long, deep breath and uttered an act of total surrender to God. It didn't matter if he ever spoke again. It didn't matter that people would never hear God's message from him. It didn't matter what he did for the rest of his life.

It didn't matter.

It didn't matter.

It didn't matter.

A few minutes later, Father sat up on the gurney and began to put his shoes back on. The doctor rushed over and said, "Where are you going? You need to lie down!"

Father spoke clearly and distinctly, as if nothing had happened.

"I'm cured, doctor. I'm going home."

We are made for total surrender

Something happens when we surrender and just trust; suddenly we are caught up into another world that we know is where we should have been all along.

Fear goes away.

A weight is lifted.

Hope returns.

Peace rushes in.

And—despite troubling circumstances—even *a lightness of heart returns.*

I can't help but think of the beauty of the marital act when there is genuine trust. The first time a woman is in arms that she knows will keep her safe, kissing lips that will profess true love, she can relax and open to receive all the gifts, joys, and pleasures her husband desires to give her. That surrender releases her own loving response so that it flows out of her like honey, back into the heart of her husband.

But without trust, sex becomes guarded, disconnected, incomplete, merely lustful, or even tedious. A woman's body—like her heart—was not made to open up to anything but real love.

This is the whole of the Christian faith: God desires that each soul live virtuously in the world with others but that she surrender completely to his touch and reserve that most intimate part of her heart for him alone.

In my talks and books, I share the "Seven Stages of Divine Romance." In drawing on this spousal analogy found in Scripture—where the soul is the bride and God is the husband—you can gain some powerful insight to your relationship with the Lord, especially about trust. Every romance progresses through seven stages, but many get stuck along the way, never advancing to the fulfillment of love. Or worse, never making it to heaven.

In this beautiful and intimate bridal imagery, some souls (including men, too, who are the bride of Christ) have "dated" or been "engaged" to God but have never "gone all the way." They have never fully surrendered every part of their life to his tender care. Why?

Lack of trust.

No woman in her right mind (that being the key phrase!) would make herself completely vulnerable to a man she did not trust to love her rightly and protect her fiercely. The truth is that most of us love God and are deeply devoted to him, worship him in his divinity, receive him in the Sacraments . . . but still do not fully trust him with some very important parts of or lives. Those fears serve as protective barriers, but they block the fullness of divine life in us.

Sometimes we can experience moments of full surrender, but when fears creep in, we take it back. If you're like me, you have come a long way in your relationship with God, but you also know it will likely be a lifetime of continued efforts with his grace to advance in holiness. He will never give up on you, so don't be discouraged or give up on him.

Oh Jesus, I surrender myself to you

What should we remember about trust?

There are people to whom you should not "surrender" or they will eat you alive.

Your trust in another is a gift and should not be given away indiscriminately.

If you can't trust others, you can *trust God.*

Surrendering to God's care is the greatest act of love we can make—if not completely in our emotions, at least in our will. Even when we do not fully understand and even when it hurts. There are many beautiful Catholic prayers and litanies that help us make continual acts of surrender to Our Lord, including "The Novena of Surrender:"

Novena of Surrender to the Will of God

(Author: Father Don Dolindo Ruotolo 1882–1970)

Day 1

Why do you confuse yourselves by worrying?
Leave the care of your affairs to me
and everything will be peaceful.
I say to you in truth that every act of true,
blind, complete surrender to me
produces the effect that you desire
and resolves all difficult situations.

(Repeat the following prayer ten times.)

O Jesus, I surrender myself to you, take care of everything!

(The rest of the Novena can be found at surrenderprayer. weebly.com.)

Then *listen*.
Let him *lead* you.
Let him *love* you.
And *let go* of fear.

Reflections

- What thoughts and emotions come to you when you think of "surrender?"
- Has someone ever deeply betrayed your trust? How did it affect you?
- When was a moment you have surrendered to God? How did it feel?

PART 6

Sitting at the Fire

Hope is sure of pardon and is without fear of being punished. . . . Hope is able to be on the lookout for the promised reward.

—St. John Cassian, *Conferences*

16

Releasing the Shame

For he whose sin is forgiven has nothing whereof to be ashamed.

—St. Ambrose, *Concerning Repentance*

"Simon, son of John, do you love me more than these?"

I imagine Peter took a slow, deep breath before he replied to Jesus.

It was after the Resurrection, and Peter and some of the other disciples had been fishing in the Sea of Tiberias late into the night and had caught nothing. Just as morning had broken, they'd seen Jesus on the shore but didn't recognize him. When the Lord hollered out to throw their nets back into the water and their nets were suddenly filled with a huge catch, they then knew who he was. Now the Master had beckoned them to bring some fish and come join him for breakfast where he had prepared a warm and crackling charcoal fire.

It had been around another charcoal fire where Peter, warming his hands but in fear for his life, had earlier denied Jesus three times. Upon hearing the cock crow, as Jesus foretold, Peter had been filled with such shame and regret that "he went out and wept bitterly" (Mt 26:75). To make his shame worse, in the Gospel of Luke (22:61), we read that "the Lord turned and looked at him."

And now Jesus had turned and was again looking directly at Peter. The Lord was preparing to do a beautiful restorative work in his dear friend's heart that morning.

> When they had finished breakfast, Jesus said to Simon Peter, "Simon, son of John, do you love me more than these?" He said to him, "Yes, Lord; you know that I love you." He said to him, "Feed my lambs." A second time he said to him, "Simon, son of John, do you love me?" He said to him, "Yes, Lord; you know that I love

you." He said to him, "Tend my sheep."
He said to him the third time, "Simon,
son of John, do you love me?" Peter was
grieved because he said to him the third
time, "Do you love me?" And he said to
him, "Lord, you know everything; you
know that I love you." Jesus said to him,
"Feed my sheep." (Jn 21:15–17)

For each of the three prior betrayals—sometimes
called Peter's "triple treason"—Jesus offers Peter
an opportunity for redemption. With each dec-
laration of love, Jesus commissions him to share
in his saving work. And after having said all of
this, Jesus wraps it up with a new *Follow Me*.
This, too, recalls an event from their past—their
first meeting!—and transfigures it.

It's encouraging to see that Jesus called Peter
a "rock" long before he had matured in his faith.
That should give us hope and help us focus on
the good in us rather than the shameful things
we regret. The Lord still wants to assure of us of
his love and help cool our shame; he also wants
us to do the same in our relationships. Some of
the things to remember about shame are:

Shame and guilt are different

Both shame and guilt keep people on the straight and narrow, avoiding sinful thoughts or behavior, but there is a difference:

Guilt is an interior regret and something you can experience alone. It's your conscience telling you that you have failed; something you've thought, said, or did was wrong. With guilt, you care more about your responsibility to God and others and your actions toward them. The remedy for guilt is atonement and repentance, apology and forgiveness.

Shame is an interior fear of rejection or condemnation (real or perceived) by others for your action or inaction. It's kind of a "false guilt" based more on what people think of you than what you did or didn't do. With shame, you often care more about how others see you than what you did or did not do. The remedy for shame is to be assured of being loved despite your failures.

Sometimes you can feel one or the other; at other times, you can feel both. At the fire, Jesus did not accept, minimize, or tolerate Peter's betrayals—they were grave and serious offenses against love and truth. But Jesus cooled Peter's burning shame when he offered him the remedies for shame and guilt:

1. assurance of his love and forgiveness,
2. a chance to repent and turn away from his betrayals, and
3. an invitation to atone, leave his sins behind, and go higher.

This is what it means to be Catholic in our relationships: to hate the sin, love the sinner, and call them into the great adventure of following Christ into holiness.

Shame comes from feeling unworthy and unloved

The movie *The Gospel of John*, in its three-hour version, is word-for-word the Gospel of John. Nothing added, nothing deleted. It's exquisite. The scene at the morning fire is tender and touching and you can see the pained look on Peter's face when the Lord asks if he loves him. But in a most tender gesture, Jesus leans in close to Peter and takes his hands and continues to assure him of his love.

Our Lord has done that for me as well.

It was in the Sacrament of Reconciliation; I was at a Theology of the Body retreat and had been suddenly and deeply convicted of past sins of impurity that I had never really confessed. They were decades old, but I knew I needed to come before God in his Sacrament, own them, and release them. One of the attending priests agreed to hear my confession.

The priest led me to a side room, closed the door, and brought two chairs together, facing each other. I sat down opposite him, so close my knees nearly touched his, and I took a slow, deep breath. Father kissed his stole, placed it around his neck, and asked me when I had made my last confession. I told him, bowed my head in sorrow, and began.

"Bless me, Father, for I have sinned."

I started when I was in high school. Boys had moved their hands into places they should not have, and (afraid of rejection and hungry for love) I allowed it. As I continued my list of sexual sins, vivid memories of male hands came flooding back. With each relationship, I saw and could "feel" man's hands on me, pushing back against my weak boundaries. Hands that promised and then lied. Hands that violated. Hands that I had always hoped would hold me, protect me, and bless me. Instead they used me—and I learned to use back.

In my mind, I knew the Lord loved and forgave me, but in my emotions, I was sinking into the dark shame of my past.

My head still bowed, eyes closed, hands folded in my lap, and confession nearly over. I was startled to suddenly feel strong, warm man's hands tenderly envelop mine.

Father had reached out and taken both of my hands in his and held them tight for what was probably a few seconds but seemed much longer. Then he laid his hands on my head and spoke the words of absolution.

"God, the Father of all Mercies . . ."

I was flooded with healing love. The shame was gone, and only perfect peace was in its place.

Father had not known my inner thoughts or seen the images flashing before me, but Jesus did. Through his priest, Our Lord forever redeemed my memories of hurtful hands. If old memories come to haunt me, Jesus's hands will be there instead. And I will forever love and pray for that priest. If we confess our sins, he is faithful and just and will forgive us our sins and purify us from all unrighteousness (1 Jn 19).

Let him reach out and touch you.

Reflections

- What was a moment of shame from your childhood?
- What was a moment of shame from your adult life?
- What happened in your last confession?

17

Seeking Forgiveness

As often as I look upon the cross, so often will I forgive with all my heart.

—St. Faustina Kowalska, *Divine Mercy in My Soul*

This lovely definition of forgiveness is often attributed to Mark Twain: *Forgiveness is the fragrance that the violet sheds on the heel that has crushed it.*

There's no reliable evidence that Twain originated it, and, in fact, there is a long history in literature of similar poetry with different aromatic plants. Another version from an 1847 Sunday School lesson:

The sandal-tree perfumes, when riven,

The axe that laid it low;
Let him who hopes to be forgiven,
Forgive and bless his foe.

A beautiful sentiment, isn't it? But when *you* have been betrayed and repeatedly used, wounded, or defiled in a relationship, it's *you* that might like to lay the ax low into someone else's neck. We've all seen or heard about the parents or families in court who have forgiven a family member's murderer. We deeply admire them and pray to be similarly free of resentments but—face it—forgiveness is not easy.

Big offenses require big forgiveness

In my decades of work with those wounded by divorce, there are a handful of true-life stories I will never forget. A few years ago, I was facilitating a day-long parish retreat for the separated and divorced, and in our discussion of depression, one sad and tired-looking woman admitted she was depressed because she was struggling with unforgiveness.

"I just don't know if I can ever forgive him . . ." She didn't offer any details.

"We're here for you," I assured her quietly. "After lunch, we will get more into forgiveness."

Later that afternoon, I provided the group with a long list of what forgiveness is and is not (and you have it at the end of this chapter) and then opened it up for discussion.

I just can't forgive my wife for driving us into bankruptcy with her shopping addiction. We lost everything, including our home, and now she has some new boyfriend footing the bill.

Of course, heads shook in mild disbelief and nodded in understanding.

I struggle with forgiveness because of my husband's affairs. I got a divorce and *a sexually transmitted disease out of it!*

How do I forgive my *husband? He says he just fell out of love with me and needed a change. After thirty-eight years?*

Finally, the tired woman stood.

"Well, I didn't say it earlier. But I am really having a hard time with forgiveness."

She paused, and we all gave her that moment.

"Do you want to share?" I asked her gently.

"Well . . . my husband fought me for custody of our two girls. He finally told me that if he couldn't have them, neither would I. *He shot and killed both of them, and then shot and killed himself.*"

We all froze in shock and horror.

"How do I forgive him?" she added plaintively. Everyone in the room was silent.

How indeed?

For all of us, no matter how violent the offense, forgiveness only comes with time, grace, and our humble "yes."

Forgiveness is not optional

Forgiveness is not an option if you want freedom, happiness, peace, and eternal salvation. Jesus was clear when he told the parable of the unforgiving servant (Mt 18:23–35) who was grated unmerited mercy and forgiveness from his Master but then turned around and refused mercy (forgiveness) to a man who owed him a debt. When the Master found out, he had the man handed over to the jailers. Reciprocity is vital in God's economy.

Linda (not her real name, of course) was hell-bent on making my life miserable. I knew that behind her negative reactions to me was some kind of fear, but the understanding didn't make it any easier in dealing with her. She spread false public rumors, tried to get me fired, and caused the loss of some of my clients and a hefty chunk of income. I knew I had to forgive her, but part of me wanted to crush her.

One evening, I was going through some old photos and there she was in a church, standing before a priest for a blessing. I started to smirk to myself, but something stopped me. It was as if time froze, and as I stared at the photo, the priest came alive and his head turned around to look out of the photo right at me!

Then he turned into Jesus and "spoke" to me.

"Rose, you are my precious daughter, but she is too. *I love her so tenderly.* Won't *you* love her too?"

Sigh.

That's all I had to hear. *Yes, Lord, of course I will.* And I did. Resentment was released in me at that moment and I was keenly aware of a simple way to hate the sin and love the sinner: by remembering who others are—made in his image and beloved by God. You don't have to forget the reality of the offense. In fact, you may still have to deal with it. But *you let go* of your pride, your need to be right, your need to be heard, and your need for justice. Or revenge!

Forgiveness

What forgiveness is NOT

It's not approving of what the other person did. You have the right, and often the responsibility, to express disapproval of wrongdoing.

It's not accepting what the other person did. You must not tolerate improper or sinful behavior or attitudes. In fact, if you do, you become party to the problem.

It's not excusing or justifying the other person's behavior. You don't always have to find reasons why your child, spouse, or friend did what he or she did that hurt you.

It's not staying friendly with the other person. If someone continually lies, hurts, or abuses you, you don't have to be his or her friend. Jesus told his disciples to shake the dust off their feet and leave town when people rejected them. And he didn't insist they become buddies with the Pharisees.

It's not forgetting. Remembering helps us stay safe, but we should tuck the memory away and keep our focus on whatever is good.[8]

It's not continuing to trust the other person. You are not obligated to trust anyone. In fact, sometimes that's stupid, or worse . . . dangerous. Trust and respect have to be earned. We can't always trust man, but we can always trust God.

What forgiveness IS

It's seeing the other person through Jesus's eyes. He sees all the flaws and loves that person anyway. Are you a better judge than Jesus?

It's trusting God to take care of justice. You might withhold forgiveness because you don't believe God will deal with the hurtful person properly. You may want to punish him or her since you don't think God will. Or you don't think he will act soon enough for you.

It's releasing the hurt in your own heart. Holding on to unforgiveness keeps you stuck at

---

[8]   See Phil 4:8.

the greatest point of your pain. Forgiving takes the needle out of your own heart.

It's choosing to obey God. Regardless of how you feel, or all the reasons and rationalizations why you should or shouldn't forgive, God commands it. If you love him, you will keep his commandments. It's that simple.

It's opening the door to receiving forgiveness from God for your own sins. Scripture says that if you don't forgive, you make it impossible for God to forgive you. Remember "Forgive us our debts, as we also have forgiven our debtors"? The *as* means "just like." God will forgive us just like we forgive others. That means if we don't, he can't either.

Reflections

- Do you find forgiveness easy or difficult? Why?
- Is there someone you need to forgive right now? What is holding you back?
- Who have you hurt? Have you sought their forgiveness? Why or why not?

18

Letting God Lead

*Your tears were collected by the angels and
were placed in a gold chalice, and you will find
them when you present yourself before God.*

—Padre Pio, *Send Me Your Guardian Angel*

As a child, I loved walking to Our Lady of
the Assumption Elementary School—there
were so many interesting sights and pleasures
along the way!

Sometimes I would pick roses from a neighbor's front yard to give to my teacher. Once, I
stopped along the way at someone's property to
help myself to a ripe ruby-red pomegranate but
didn't realize I'd left my math book under the
tree. Later that morning, the woman who owned
the house delivered my book to my classroom.

179

Embarrassed at being caught, I also wondered how in the world Sister had known I'd stolen a pomegranate—until she pointed out the tiny dark red splatters on my white uniform middy.

But the worst memory of walking to school was the day I lost my first filling.

God is your loving Father

"Bye, Mom!" I hollered as I grabbed my plaid lunch pail and navy-blue uniform sweater and slammed the front door.

On my way to the third grade, I headed down El Camino Avenue to the stoplight, where I'd cross carefully and continue five more blocks to the playground. About halfway there I opened my lunch box and took out a shiny, green apple. CHOMP!

As I was chewing, I bit down onto something hard and unfamiliar, so I spat it out into my hand. With horror, I realized it was a dental filling, and my tongue probed around until it found a huge hole in one of my molars. It scared me.

Oh NO, I thought, *what now?*

I knew I'd have to go to our family dentist, Dr. Worsely. I hated his office, where the room temperature was barely above freezing, and the air held the faint scent of burning teeth and oral antiseptic. The last time I'd been in his chair, and I heard the high-pitched whine of the metal drill, I cowered and squirmed and protested so much that he slapped me across the face to make me sit still.

I don't remember anything after that except that I *never* wanted to back there again. Ever!

Now here I was at the street intersection, not knowing whether to cross or not. Mom wasn't home; she'd left right after I had to go downtown on errands. Dad was at work, so our house was empty. Should I keep going on to school? What would Sister even know about my huge trauma? Did nuns have fillings? Would everyone make fun of me? I couldn't move forward or go back. I froze, holding back tears.

A little voice inside me said, *Rosie, you have to find someone to help you!* Back in those days it was relatively safe to approach a stranger and ask for help. So, I looked ahead at the cars that were stopped at the traffic light. It was a warm spring morning and the car right in front had its windows rolled down. *I could call out to the driver and he would hear me*, I thought, but before I could say "Excuse me, mister," I realized that car was my dad's, and the man sitting in the driver's seat was my father!

"DADDY!" I screamed, running to the side of the car, and bursting into tears.

My father was surprised to see me, but he pulled slowly over to the curb, got out, and scooped me up in his arms. I buried my head in his chest and heaved uncontrollably. All he could hear were muffled sounds of "wah-h-h . . . filling . . . apple . . . don't make me go there . . . wah-h-h-h."

When I finally calmed down, Dad told me everything would be alright, and somehow, I knew it would. In my father's arms, the truth about having to see the dentist again became a manageable problem instead of the end of the world. Daddy always made everything okay and I didn't have to worry anymore.

This might sound like a childish story that has nothing to do with adults trying to rebuild or recover from broken relationships. But at the heart of this true story is a central truth to your rebuilding: *God is a loving Father who can be trusted.* He *will* help you redesign and rebuild—or even appropriately let go of—your relationships.

God will make a way for love

Mom was days near death. She didn't recognize me or anyone and could not speak. I knew she would be gone soon and was thinking back on our long-troubled relationship. One day years before, she had looked me right in the eyes and declared, "You are my enemy."

What? Enemy? That was pretty harsh, I thought.

At that point, I'd had no idea of the degree of resentment Mom had carried toward me. It was painful but clarifying. With the help of my spiritual director, I had been able to confess my own part in things, seek forgiveness from Mom, and forgive her for her part. At least we had made some small amount of peace with each other a few years before her final illnesses.

I sat at the edge of her bed in the hospital

thinking, *What can I give her that would bring her some small joy?*

"Can I get you anything, Mom?"

No response. Just a blank stare.

"Would you like me to stay a little bit longer?"

No response.

I continued to just sit with her in silence.

Then I remembered her love for Ovaltine and, particularly, for chocolate malts. When we had been to the ice-cream store, she had always ordered extra-malt.

"Mom, can I go get you a chocolate malt?"

Surprisingly, her eyes widened. I took it as a yes.

"*Okay*! Mom, I'm going to go get you a shake and will be back soon."

I hurriedly grabbed my purse and keys and drove to Baskin-Robbins. I ordered extra malt.

Back at the hospital, I stood alongside the head of her bed, holding her shake and guiding the straw to her mouth. As she sucked the chocolatey drink, her eyelids lowered in that contented milk-coma that kids often get when they are drinking their bottle.

Suddenly I was back on the day Mom had tenderly given me that Ovaltine bottle.

I sat down on the edge of her bed, gave her my most loving look, and without thinking, I stroked her forehead, brushing back her silver hair.

Relationships take work, but they bring rest.

Relationships are painful, but they are worth it.

If you don't get lost in relationships, you will find your way to heaven.

God will always open a door and make a way for love.

Don't give up.

Reflections

- What did you learn about love from your parents?
- How has God proven to be a loving Father to you?
- What relationship would you like him to bless right now?

Forty Pearls of Wisdom

Spiritual Works of Mercy

Listening

1 – Let go of any agendas
2 - Stop talking
3 - Remove distractions
4 - Convey interest
5 - Give them time
6 - Try to understand (you don't have to agree)
7 - Pay attention to body language
8 - Don't interrupt, defend, or fix
9 – Ask for clarification
10 – Be patient

Leading

1 – Ground yourself in truth
2 – **Counsel the doubtful***
3 – Stay appropriately detached
4 – Stay humble

5 – Ask questions
6 – Set and enforce boundaries
7 – **Instruct the ignorant***
8 – Be respectful (not tolerant)
9 – **Admonish the sinner***
10 – Let them fall

Loving

1 – Let God love you first
2 – Desire the greatest good for them (holiness)
3 – Be willing to lose in order to win
4 – **Comfort the afflicted***
5 – Protect their dignity
6 – Respect their free will
7 – Give voice to your love
8 – Give them time and space
9 – **Pray for them***
10 - Keep the door open

Letting Go

1 – Face your fears
2 – Stop trying to fix or control
3 – Rearrange the relationship

4 - Communicate clearly
5 – Create necessary distance
6 – Grieve the loss
7 – **Forgive easily*** (include yourself)
8 – Seek forgiveness for your part
9 – **Bear wrongs patiently***
10 – Hang on to hope